BOSOMS AND NEGLECT

Revised Edition

BY JOHN GUARE

★

DRAMATISTS
PLAY SERVICE
INC.

BOSOMS AND NEGLECT
Copyright © Revised, 1999, St. Jude Productions, Inc.
Copyright © 1980, St. Jude Productions, Inc.

ALL RIGHTS RESERVED

CAUTION: Professionals and amateurs are hereby warned that performance of BOSOMS AND NEGLECT is subject to a royalty. It is fully protected under the copyright laws of the United States of America, and of all countries covered by the International Copyright Union (including the Dominion of Canada and the rest of the British Commonwealth), and of all countries covered by the Pan-American Copyright Convention, the Universal Copyright Convention, the Berne Convention, and of all countries with which the United States has reciprocal copyright relations. All rights, including professional/amateur stage rights, motion picture, recitation, lecturing, public reading, radio broadcasting, television, video or sound recording, all other forms of mechanical or electronic reproduction, such as CD-ROM, CD-I, DVD, information storage and retrieval systems and photocopying, and the rights of translation into foreign languages, are strictly reserved. Particular emphasis is placed upon the matter of readings, permission for which must be secured from the Author's representative in writing.

The stage performance rights in BOSOMS AND NEGLECT (other than first class rights) are controlled exclusively by the DRAMATISTS PLAY SERVICE, INC., 440 Park Avenue South, New York, N.Y. 10016. No professional or non-professional performance of the Play (excluding first class professional performance) may be given without obtaining in advance the written permission of the DRAMATISTS PLAY SERVICE, INC., and paying the requisite fee.

Inquiries concerning all other rights should be addressed to Kay Collyer & Boose, 1 Dag Hammarskjold Plaza, New York, N.Y. 10017. Attn: R. Andrew Boose, Esq.

SPECIAL NOTE

Anyone receiving permission to produce BOSOMS AND NEGLECT is required to give credit to the Author as sole and exclusive Author of the Play on the title page of all programs distributed in connection with performances of the Play and in all instances in which the title of the Play appears for purposes of advertising, publicizing or otherwise exploiting the Play and/or a production thereof. The name of the Author must appear on a separate line, in which no other name appears, immediately beneath the title and in size of type equal to 50% of the largest, most prominent letter used for the title of the Play. No person, firm or entity may receive credit larger or more prominent than that accorded the Author.

SPECIAL NOTE ON SONGS AND RECORDINGS

For performance of the songs, arrangements and recordings mentioned in this Play that are protected by copyright, the permission of the copyright owners must be obtained; or other songs, arrangements and recordings in the public domain substituted.

For Adele

The final revision of BOSOMS AND NEGLECT was produced by Signature Theater (Founding Artistic Director, James Houghton; Managing Director, Thomas C. Proehl; Elliot Fox, Associate Director) in New York City, on December 13, 1998. It was directed by Nicholas Martin; the set design was by James Noone; the lighting design was by Frances Aronson; and the sound design was by Red Ramona. The cast was as follows:

HENNY	Mary Louise Wilson
SCOOPER	David Aaron Baker; later, B.D. Wong
DEIRDRE	Katie Finneran

BOSOMS AND NEGLECT, directed by Mel Shapiro, was produced on Broadway by Bernard Gersten and John Wulp, in association with Marc Howard, at the Longacre Theatre, in New York City, on May 3, 1979. (An initial engagement at the Goodman Theatre, Chicago, Illinois [Gregory Mosher, Artistic Director], opened March 1, 1979.) The set design was by John Wulp; the costume design was by Willa Kim; and the lighting design was by Jennifer Tipton. The cast was as follows:

HENNY	Kate Reid
SCOOPER	Paul Rudd
DEIRDRE	Marian Mercer

Revisions were made for a subsequent production at the New York Theater Workshop, in New York City, on March 26, 1986, with Anne Meara as HENNY, Richard Cavanaugh as SCOOPER, and April Shawhan as DEIRDRE. It was directed by Larry Arrick.

CHARACTERS

HENNY
SCOOPER
DEIRDRE

SCENE

ACT ONE: Deirdre's apartment. The East Side of Manhattan.
ACT TWO: Henny's hospital room.

BOSOMS AND NEGLECT

ACT ONE

Two pools of light. In one, a man, Scooper, late thirties, trim, fit, is curled up on a couch in agony. In the other, a woman, Deirdre, sits calmly, strong.

DEIRDRE. Try. Try.
SCOOPER. No …
DEIRDRE. Tell me. You're in a safe place.
SCOOPER. I … found a doctor who'd make house calls. *(The lights change. Scooper sits up. We are in his story. He stands, holding an empty, washed mayonnaise jar and calls out, cheerily.)* I found a doctor who makes house calls. *(In darkness, Henny sings in a raucous voice a pop tune along the lines of "When the Red Red Robin Comes Bob Bob Bobbin' Along.")** Talk about Mission Impossible. He'll be here in about fifteen minutes.
HENNY. Oh God. God. Oh God. *(Henny comes forward, her fingers in her ears, still singing. She is old. She is blind. She is terrified.)*
SCOOPER. This house-call doctor wants you to fill up a jar so he can take it to the lab. I have to bring it up to the pharmacy on Eighty-second Street. So can you fill this up?
HENNY. I don't have to go.
SCOOPER. *Now* you don't have to go. *(To Deirdre.)* Now she didn't have to go.
DEIRDRE. Cystitis?
SCOOPER. *(To Henny.)* Cystitis?
HENNY. I don't have any cystitis.
SCOOPER. Don't go screaming and crying and shaking so hard. He can't get a look at you if you're screaming and crying and shaking so hard. I told him it burns when you pee. I told him it's probably cystitis. Don't close your ears and hum.

* See Special Note on Songs and Recordings on copyright page.

HENNY. My bladder fell out.
SCOOPER. This magic doctor says "What does this mean, her bladder fell out." I said "That's what she says, her bladder fell out."
HENNY. My bladder fell out.
SCOOPER. *(To Deirdre.)* It burnt when she peed.
HENNY. It burns when I pee.
SCOOPER. *(Hands Henny the bottle.)* The doctor has a Spanish accent so when he comes, don't go running out because he's a foreigner. He's a real Latin Lover type is what he sounds like. Take the bottle! And don't go falling in love with him when you hear his Latin accent.
HENNY. *(Feeling the bottle.)* You'd have to be a contortionist in a circus to fit on this. What's wrong with you?
SCOOPER. What's wrong with me who finds a doctor who makes house calls? Have you got a juice bottle?
HENNY. My bladder fell out. I can feel it. Give me your hand. Touch it. Oh God. You can feel it. *(Henny grabs for his hand.)*
SCOOPER. *(Pulls back.)* I'm not the doctor. Don't go using me as the doctor. I'm not going to touch you there. *(To Deirdre.)* I went out of the room. *(Scooper goes into the dark.)*
HENNY. This doctor's going to lock me up when he sees me. When he sees this bladder.
SCOOPER. *(Off.)* The doctor's not the enemy.
HENNY. How do you know? You never saw him before. He's going to run out of here screaming when he sees me. *(Scooper returns with a quart-size juice jar.)*
SCOOPER. Doctors don't run out on patients. Crazy patients do the running out so the doctors can't treat them, fix them. Fill this jar. *(He puts the jar in her hands.)*
HENNY. It's ... it's not just my bladder.
SCOOPER. *(To Deirdre.)* Over on the table, I suddenly saw a box. *(To Henny.)* Why does an eighty-three-year-old woman have a giant box of Super Kotex? You're not having reverse change of life? Medical marvels. What is this Kotex doing here?
HENNY. I thought it would go away.
SCOOPER. What would go away?
HENNY. I prayed to Saint Jude and said Saint Jude Patron

Saint of Lost Causes, Patron Saint of the Impossible, Patron Saint of the Damned, take this away from me.
SCOOPER.   Take what away from you?
HENNY.   It bleeds and bleeds and I put Kotex over it and stand in front of the window all night in the dark looking up waving a statue of Saint Jude over it so it'll dry by the morning. But it never dries. It never stops bleeding. I sent out for more Kotex. It never stops bleeding. *(He grabs her.)* You're hurting my arm!
SCOOPER.   What never stops bleeding?
HENNY.   I never would've told you about the other incident, except my insides are falling out and I can't pee and I told you and I could cut my tongue out because it don't hurt that much when I pee. I could live with it. It's not so bad.
SCOOPER.   This other incident?
HENNY.   It doesn't hurt. If I could see, I could see it was nothing. But I can't see so I make it up in my mind that it's more than it is, you see.
SCOOPER.   Where is this incident?
HENNY.   It's not hide-and-seek, for Christ's sake. I haven't got it hidden in the back of the stove. It's here. It's me. The incident is me.
SCOOPER.   How long?
HENNY.   Not long.
SCOOPER.   Deal straight. How long?
HENNY.   It started in a way I could notice the day you and Valerie and Ted came out here.
SCOOPER.   That was two years ago.
HENNY.   It started that day.
SCOOPER.   What started that day?
HENNY.   The skin broke that day.
SCOOPER.   Skin where?
HENNY.   It's not important.
SCOOPER.   What skin broke?
HENNY.   I can deal with this. My Kotex and Saint Jude and I are very happy. I don't have to pee. If I can just work it so I don't have to pee, I'm all right.
SCOOPER.   *(To Deirdre.)* The doorbell rang. *(To Henny.)* He's

here. The doctor is here.
HENNY. Send him away.
SCOOPER. We'll hold you down and strip you and find this incident.
HENNY. It feels better. Go away.
SCOOPER. What skin broke?
HENNY. *(Impatiently.)* Oh God. Here. *(She opens her blouse. He steps back, horrified. Deirdre stands.)* It doesn't look so bad. Does it? Real false alarm. Girl who cried wolf. One day something will be wrong with me and you won't bother to help me because I dragged you out here once before for a little nothing. You're too young to have problems. I don't want to burden you with my problems. You want to send out to that new Italian deli for shrimp salad? They use real shrimp. None of those little plastic pinkies. I buy it to last two days and it's gone before I'm even ready for dinner.
SCOOPER. Oh dear God. Oh Christ. Jesus H. fucking Christ.
HENNY. There is no reason for such language. Saint Jude does not like it. Want me to go to the door and tell the doctor to go away? False alarm time? I'll give him five dollars. See my system? The five-dollar bills have one safety pin in them. The tens I have the girl put two safety pins in. The ones are on their own. *(The door chime sounds.)* Tell him April Fool. Say Saint Jude helped a supposed lost cause make a miraculous recovery.
SCOOPER. Doctor, you'd better get in here.
HENNY. No! *(Henny retreats into the dark. Deirdre stands. The back cyclorama is hot orange. The light streams into her wonderful apartment carved out of an elegant brownstone in the East Sixties, bookcases overflowing with books. Stacks of books are everywhere but still there is a sense of order. Calm, peace. She uses a section of the room as an office, with Jiffy mailing envelopes, wrapping paper, twine, a stamp machine, and a scale. Deirdre is in her thirties. Very beautiful. Very intense. She is very cool, dressed in white. She holds a glass of wine and leans forward, listening to Scooper. He sits on the couch, trying to be very rational. He wears a summer suit. His packed suitcase is by the door.)*
SCOOPER. Imagine a peach that had an enormous bite taken out of it.

DEIRDRE. Oh Christ.
SCOOPER. I'm not finished. Then. Then.
DEIRDRE. Calm.
SCOOPER. Was left in the back of a disconnected refrigerator for the winter months and you come back in the spring and open the icebox door and find the peach rotted where the bite was taken out. This poison gauze. This penicillin rot-mold. You could put your fist into the hole in her breast. The cancer was that deep.
DEIRDRE. Wait.
SCOOPER. She stood there, her blouse off. It's not so bad, she keeps saying. It is not so bad.
DEIRDRE. It's impossible. What you're describing.
SCOOPER. I saw it.
DEIRDRE. Cancer works slowly.
SCOOPER. I am telling you — I can't believe you are not believing me. I pour this out and your response is ...
DEIRDRE. I'm not saying you're hallucinating. I'm saying cancer works inside, silently. Not like some horror show in a drive-in.
SCOOPER. She had so neglected herself that the disease was sick of not being noticed. The disease finally burst through her skin. The ulceration was like this screaming flesh, this breast — screaming how loud do you have to go to get noticed?
DEIRDRE. Oh Christ.
SCOOPER. The good part about being that old the metabolism moves so slowly that the cancer takes just that much longer.
DEIRDRE. And she had no medical aid?
SCOOPER. Sure. For two years, she's been laying Kotex over the wound, waving this tan plastic statue of Saint Jude, Patron of Lost Causes, over this small, expanding cavity in her chest, standing all night in the dark privacy of her open window so the midnight air would dry it out.
DEIRDRE. You never noticed?
SCOOPER. I never saw her.
DEIRDRE. In two years?
SCOOPER. She only likes talking on the phone. I can't see

her. She can't see me. Gives her equal footing.
DEIRDRE. But her bladder —
SCOOPER. It was her uterus.
DEIRDRE. Oh dear God.
SCOOPER. It fell out.
DEIRDRE. Oh no.
SCOOPER. Eighty-three-year-old muscles give out.
DEIRDRE. But still —
SCOOPER. The doctor who made the house call said This woman is finished. This woman will not make it through the day. It's not so bad. Girl who cried wolf. False alarm. I paid off the doctor. Got Doctor James on the phone. Got her up to New York-Presbyterian.
DEIRDRE. The best.
SCOOPER. Doctor James waiting right there. He had a bed waiting, the best surgeon all lined up to see her.
DEIRDRE. That was yesterday?
SCOOPER. That was yesterday.
DEIRDRE. And today she's on the table?
SCOOPER. Right now.
DEIRDRE. It makes me feel so well taken care of, like a great fringe benefit, if anything happened to me.
SCOOPER. Thanks to Doctor James.
DEIRDRE. A toast to you.
SCOOPER. To me?
DEIRDRE. To him. *(She pours wine. White. Chilled. They toast.)*
SCOOPER. After two years of lying and hiding.
DEIRDRE. You?
SCOOPER. Her. *(They sip.)*
DEIRDRE. Poor tragic lady. Outliving her friends. Standing all night at a window. Not trusting any human being enough to reach out.
SCOOPER. Don't forget the statue she's waving over her breast. Significant detail. Saint Jude. Patron of Lost Causes.
DEIRDRE. I suddenly have this image of being blind. Oh God. Never to be able to browse. I could never learn Braille. The skin on my fingers might be too tough to let the words come through.

SCOOPER.   She elected to go blind.
DEIRDRE.   You don't cast votes to be blind.
SCOOPER.   Twenty years ago she did. She marched right up to the polling booth with her glaucoma and cataracts. Her hysteria rendered her untreatable. She looked at my father and me with these eyes turning to milk, the sight curdling out of them. "You're lying to me, it's something worse. Tell me the truth. No, don't tell me the truth. Lie to me." She begged us to lie to her. We said we were telling the truth. She said that's the biggest lie. And she invented some exotic disease for herself. And she proceeded to go bonkers and embark on a series of suicide attempts as if the *Guinness Book of Records* suddenly had an opening.
DEIRDRE.   And she's still nuts?
SCOOPER.   As soon as she went blind, her mind snapped back like the price of gold. Nothing worse had gone wrong with her. She was only blind. That she could live with. You become saner much quicker than you go mad. So we had ten years of suicide attempts. And now the last ten she's been feeling her way around like a lost company of *The Miracle Worker.*
DEIRDRE.   Your father?
SCOOPER.   He stroked out along the way. One day he just short-circuited while she was eating a lightbulb ... or a knife. Stop looking at me that way.
DEIRDRE.   Do you find it so difficult taking care of another human being?
SCOOPER.   She did it herself.
DEIRDRE.   I see why you go to Doctor James.
SCOOPER.   Sight is a collaborative act, requiring subject and object working together in trust and tranquillity. You have to tell the doctor what you're seeing and if you're screaming and have flames shooting out of your ears — *(He downs his drink. He looks around at all her books.)* Are you in publishing?
DEIRDRE.   I buy and sell. From estates. First editions.
SCOOPER.   You could have two lions in front of your door.
DEIRDRE.   How old is she?
SCOOPER.   Eighty-three.
DEIRDRE.   Then why don't you let her die?

SCOOPER. Because I don't want that solution in me. She is not allowed to take that *out*. Hysteria is not an *out*. Fantasy and panic are not *out*s. I don't want the solution of suicide in my genes. I want courage in my genes. I want strength in my genes. I want seeing problems *through* in my genes. That old lady is going to stay alive and die of old age and plain old-fashioned wearing out. She is not going to be killed by an overactivity of the most valuable thing we have, our imagination. Look, you've got your own problems.
DEIRDRE. No! No! Really! I'm an ear. I love to be an ear.
SCOOPER. Still. He died right here? *(He touches her hand, gently.)* It must have been a shock.
DEIRDRE. The air conditioner was off. I thought I'd suffocate and I couldn't open any windows, all sealed shut to keep the air conditioning in, and I turned on the lights and they flickered and went out and my Walkman said it was three A.M. and a hundred degrees. I had this flashlight and picked up anything to read, just for the reading, just till it got light ... *Tess of the D'Urbervilles.*
SCOOPER. Thomas Hardy!
DEIRDRE. And Raymond leaps up. His paws cover the text. I say "Down, Raymond!" And Raymond gasped with the lack of air and falls over. Right here. Tongue hanging out. I didn't know what to do. Please let it be light! Finally it got to be time and I put on this dress and ran out.
SCOOPER. And you come back and he's gone?
DEIRDRE. Wait. The air conditioner's on.
SCOOPER. Who'd break in and kidnap a dead dog?
DEIRDRE. I see! My husband! Of course.
SCOOPER. Your husband?
DEIRDRE. Came back. Saw what happened. Took Raymond up to the animal hospital for disposal. Or the ASPCA. I'm glad that's solved. And the air conditioner turned on. Oh dear, the idea of a thief who breaks in and takes only dead pets. That's even too strange for a city of strange tales. Raymond will be back soon and all questions will be solved.
SCOOPER. Raymond? Will be back?
DEIRDRE. My husband. *(She packs a stack of books in a mailing*

box.) I really have to get back to work. Charles Dickens off to Honolulu.
SCOOPER. Your husband and your dog have the same name?
DEIRDRE. That should tell you all you need to know about my marriage.
SCOOPER. I'm sorry.
DEIRDRE. It's all over. Nothing. Really. Hand me John Updike.
SCOOPER. *(Bringing her the books.)* He must be a great help.
DEIRDRE. John Updike?
SCOOPER. Doctor James.
DEIRDRE. I read somewhere once the reason people have to go to doctors is the impossibility of the human being to say good-bye.
SCOOPER. *(Picks up some books.)* Beautiful bindings. Uncut.
DEIRDRE. I specialize in uncut.
SCOOPER. The weight. The smell. The feel. *(She takes the books away from him.)*
DEIRDRE. I was touched when you introduced yourself.
SCOOPER. You didn't say "Who is this asshole coming up to me in a Fifth Avenue bookstore?"
DEIRDRE. You're hardly a stranger.
SCOOPER. I stumbled out in the street this morning. Have a wonderful vacation, Doctor James. Don't dare ask him where he's going. Should I kiss him? Filial peck on the cheek? Yearly affection. Will he think it's a pass? Decide against. Out in the street. Jesus. Only Nine Fucking Forty Fucking Five A.M. How am I going to get through this day?
DEIRDRE. Already eighty-eight degrees.
SCOOPER. I run to a bookstore.
DEIRDRE. Not one of the big chains?
SCOOPER. No, Rizzoli's! Fifty-Seventh off Fifth. Wait for it to open. Cool. See what new books have come in since yesterday.
DEIRDRE. But it was like two degrees Celsius.
SCOOPER. Spy. Sex. Show biz. Something to turn the page.
DEIRDRE. I cannot figure out Celsius.
SCOOPER. And what do I see when I get to the corner? You. Looking in the bookstore window. Waiting for it to open. Your dress swaying slightly. How did your legs find the only breeze?

DEIRDRE. I mean, who is Celsius?
SCOOPER. You looked so healthy.
DEIRDRE. I am healthy.
SCOOPER. I didn't think you'd —
DEIRDRE. Of course I —
SCOOPER. But you moved away.
DEIRDRE. I didn't think you'd — After months of silence.
SCOOPER. I'd never seen you move. Only sit. The waiting room. Turning pages. Reading copies of *Vogue*.
DEIRDRE. Long gone out of vogue.
SCOOPER. I looked at you staring in the bookshop window and I said this woman and I share the deepest experience of a lifetime and we have never spoken a word. I have even come from a couch that was still warm from you.
DEIRDRE. You followed me.
SCOOPER. Into the bookstore. Is that woman as paralyzed as I am about Doctor James going away for a month?
DEIRDRE. Thumbing through glossy foreign magazines, looking around to see if you were following me. I pick up *Oggi, Paris Match, L'Express*.
SCOOPER. I thought you'd be glad to hear an American voice.
DEIRDRE. Just because someone speaks the same language doesn't mean you can trust them.
SCOOPER. You recognized me.
DEIRDRE. I recognized you.
SCOOPER. "Would you like to have a drink?"
DEIRDRE. "My dog's died and it's eighty-eight degrees and it's just ten A.M. and I don't know what to do."
SCOOPER. "I could help you."
DEIRDRE. "I live around the corner."
SCOOPER. "Around the corner." My God, across the street from Doctor James. I didn't think real people lived on this street. All the Mercedes lined up to haul our pains away. I thought you had to be a shrink to live here.
DEIRDRE. A friend of mine calls this street the Mental Block.
SCOOPER. A close friend?
DEIRDRE. *(Avoiding the question.)* Actually I read it.

SCOOPER. Who's with him now?
DEIRDRE. The mother who drinks.
SCOOPER. Oh Jesus. She once came out of the office and asked me for drink money right in the waiting room.
DEIRDRE. She did the same to me!
SCOOPER. I felt so guilty refusing her.
DEIRDRE. I had to have my session switched.
SCOOPER. Look! There she is!
DEIRDRE. Get down! *(Deirdre looks through binoculars she keeps hanging by the window.)*
SCOOPER. She's walking so straight.
DEIRDRE. Sober.
SCOOPER. Healed.
DEIRDRE. A cab pulls up. Out gets the pianist. He runs in, late for his appointment.
SCOOPER. He didn't play for years. That poor genius. Too crazy to play.
DEIRDRE. I have his CD. I play it all the time.
SCOOPER. I went to his concert.
DEIRDRE. I was there! *(Deirdre puts on a recording. The first movement of Scriabin's Sonata No. 4 in F# minor, Op. 30* minor fills the room. Scooper starts to speak. Deirdre shushes him. They listen intently.)*
SCOOPER. I thought: Doctor James healed this man so he can play again.
DEIRDRE. I felt the same thing.
SCOOPER. It's like we're all related.
DEIRDRE. Brothers and sisters sent in for a private loving audience with our father.
SCOOPER. *(Runs to the window, calling.)* We love you, Doctor James!!!
DEIRDRE. This is no spy turret! *(She turns off the music abruptly. Scooper comes away from the window and pours another drink.)*
SCOOPER. You must know so much about him.
DEIRDRE. I know he's got a wife.
SCOOPER. Oh, I knew that.
DEIRDRE. Poor Doctor James.

* See Special Note on Songs and Recordings on copyright page.

SCOOPER. Poor?

DEIRDRE. That tragic marriage.

SCOOPER. Did he tell you he had a tragic marriage?

DEIRDRE. How could he understand my pain if he didn't have his own? I hear it. There in his voice. That tormented way his fingers rub that birthmark on his hand. Talk about Rorschach tests. I never thought I had any imagination at all until I saw Doctor James' wine-colored birthmark ... like a magic token transforming me into whatever I want to be. Clouds. Scudding by in the birthmark.

SCOOPER. What birthmark?

DEIRDRE. On his hand.

SCOOPER. Which hand?

DEIRDRE. I lie like this. Look over like this. Yes, the left hand.

SCOOPER. I never noticed any birthmark.

DEIRDRE. Did you notice FDR was in a wheelchair?

SCOOPER. Are you calling Doctor James a cripple?

DEIRDRE. It's the most obvious thing about him.

SCOOPER. You see a spot from luncheon. And you romanticize the coagulation into a birthmark.

DEIRDRE. I have seen that birthmark every day for the past — *number* of years and it is impossible to spill that much gravy in the selfsame spot for the past — *number* of years. Let's not make this one of those events like the song in Gigi — "I Remember It Well" — based on *(Scooper joins in on:)*

DEIRDRE and SCOOPER. Colette!

DEIRDRE. — where we talk about the same thing and have completely different perceptions of it. You have your Doctor James.

SCOOPER. I have my Doctor James.

DEIRDRE. I have my birthmarks. You keep of him whatever you want.

SCOOPER. All I ever see of Doctor James are his wing-tip shoes. I love the guy, but I hate his wing-tip shoes. They're like shoes that belong to some CIA agent.

DEIRDRE. How can you see his wing-tips?

SCOOPER. He crosses his legs. I quick turn up off the couch

and look down and see the tips of his shoes.
DEIRDRE.   Hating the wings at the tips of his shoes. So fascinating. Hating the fact that Doctor James can fly.
SCOOPER.   Do you hear us romanticizing our doctor? We will have to tell him next September. He will laugh.
DEIRDRE.   You think?
SCOOPER.   You have to take risks.
DEIRDRE.   I can never forgive them for taking the month of August off.
SCOOPER.   They only do it so we won't run off to other doctors while we're away.
DEIRDRE.   As if we'd go to anyone else.
SCOOPER.   Sometimes I'll look at a friend in trouble and say Boy, if I trusted you more. Boy, do I have a doctor for you. Boy, could he tie those loose ends up in a minute.
DEIRDRE.   But you don't.
SCOOPER.   He's my secret weapon.
DEIRDRE.   That's not being selfish.
SCOOPER.   That's being protective.
DEIRDRE.   I think you'd better go.
SCOOPER.   Have I said —
DEIRDRE.   It might not be healthy talking about our doctor this way.
SCOOPER.   I think he'd be thrilled. I can't wait to tell him.
DEIRDRE.   You wouldn't dare tell him!
SCOOPER.   To bring Doctor James a new character in my life that he knows so well? You have to tell him about me. You'll bring him me. I'll bring him you. To play his version of you against my version of you. To play your me against his me. It'll be like *The Alexandria Quartet.* The air carbonated with all these realities and people! Poor Lawrence Durrell. He's become so neglected.
DEIRDRE.   Am I a major character or a minor character?
SCOOPER.   Friends are always major characters.
DEIRDRE.   Friendships are major responsibilities.
SCOOPER.   I'm a wonderful friend.
DEIRDRE.   Are you a five A.M. friend?
SCOOPER.   A five A.M. friend?

DEIRDRE. A friend you can call and say stay on the phone till it gets light.
SCOOPER. I read a book.
DEIRDRE. Sometimes a book doesn't help.
SCOOPER. You need a voice. I am a five A.M. friend. *(They look at each other, intensely.)*
DEIRDRE. Thank you for telling me about your mother, your father.
SCOOPER. *Life With Father.* Clarence Day.
DEIRDRE. I have that. I love books about families. They read to me like science fiction.
SCOOPER. You don't have any family?
DEIRDRE. They were killed when I was very young.
SCOOPER. Oh dear.
DEIRDRE. Car crash home from skiing.
SCOOPER. Stowe?
DEIRDRE. Lake Placid.
SCOOPER. Never been to Lake Placid.
DEIRDRE. I went there once.
SCOOPER. I go to Stowe.
DEIRDRE. I have this golden photo of my parents. *(She picks up a picture in a frame.)* You can see the wit in their eyes. I've learned more about life staring at this picture taken shortly before their deaths trying to riddle out their smiles. Trying to find some injunction in their wrinkled noses. At one point in my life the picture seemed spiritual. I was going to school at a convent. I became a nun for a while.
SCOOPER. You were a nun?
DEIRDRE. I mistook gratitude for a vocation.
SCOOPER. I can't imagine you as a nun.
DEIRDRE. Believe me.
SCOOPER. I'd love to see that picture.
DEIRDRE. I show it to no one. *(She closes it away in a drawer.)* Doctor James says I read so much to make up their voices reading to me. I hear what I imagine their voices to be telling me about their lives. I read only the finest works. Their voices are very golden in my ear.
SCOOPER. You must be some patient for Doctor James.

DEIRDRE. When you said you'd come from the couch warm with me, you were saying you're in analysis. You don't sit up. I mean, you're not in therapy.
SCOOPER. I'm in analysis.
DEIRDRE. I couldn't talk to you if you were just in therapy.
SCOOPER. You can talk to me.
DEIRDRE. It's so snobbish but I wouldn't have respect for you if you were in therapy — I wish you'd get away from the window. I don't want him looking up and —
SCOOPER. Remember the fat girl — did you ever get a look at her? She must've weighed in at a good four hundred pounds. I used to follow her at one time and I thought the couch would cave in —
DEIRDRE. *Ivanhoe* is an amazing book. It speaks with such an urgent clarity to today. Who'd think Sir Walter Scott would achieve —
SCOOPER. Oh my God, that wasn't you ... was it?
DEIRDRE. Good God, I don't even know who you're talking about. Is that your idea of why people to go Doctor James? He's hardly a fat farm.
SCOOPER. It's just this girl —
DEIRDRE. Why did you go to Doctor James? Weight?
SCOOPER. One little problem that needed tying up.
DEIRDRE. One little problem? No such animal.
SCOOPER. I don't want to tell you anything that'll change your impression of me —
DEIRDRE. Luckily I have no impression of you at all. *(She uncorks a wine bottle.)*
SCOOPER. I think you're right. *(He starts to go.)*
DEIRDRE. You were saying why you went —
SCOOPER. He might be angry if he knew we were —
DEIRDRE. Try lying down on the couch —
SCOOPER. I don't want to tell you —
DEIRDRE. It might make it easier.
SCOOPER. He's not lucky enough to get orphans and nuns and husbands and dogs with the same name from me.
DEIRDRE. You're afraid you're not complicated enough? How silly! It's not a competition. How often do we get to share

this magic part of our lives?
SCOOPER. It is almost religious with him.
DEIRDRE. *Pater Noster.* You and I. Brothers. Sisters.
SCOOPER. I'm an only child.
DEIRDRE. Family. That's what we are. We share family secrets.
SCOOPER. I started going to Doctor James because — *(Spots a book.)* Ahhh. *Sherlock Holmes.* Beautiful edition ... *(She takes the book from him.)* I started going to him because I was so happy.
DEIRDRE. So happy?
SCOOPER. I could live with my mother's suicide attempts and father's strokes. That was like wartime. That was easy. But for one period I stumbled inadvertently into some kind of happiness. I beamed out in this seraphic five A.M. joy Why is everything so wonderful? And the Lispenards — *my* five A.M. friends — got me Doctor James' number to find out in a few quick sessions how this wanderer had stumbled into Shangri-la and how he could stay there.
DEIRDRE. And that was —
SCOOPER. Six years ago.
DEIRDRE. Are you still happy?
SCOOPER. Well, one thing led to another. And also Val.
DEIRDRE. Valium?
SCOOPER. Valerie.
DEIRDRE. Valerie?
SCOOPER. My old lady.
DEIRDRE. You don't mean your mother.
SCOOPER. My lady. My girl. My mistress. My blood. My brain. My heart. My wonder.
DEIRDRE. How nice of her to stand by you today.
SCOOPER. No, she's up in New Hampshire putting her kids in camp. Three of them. God, I'll be a father.
DEIRDRE. They're not by you.
SCOOPER. That's a whole other saga. She had Bradley and Kim and Sophie by Cesarean so she is still tight like a young girl and you come into her so firm and then suddenly it's like coming into Saint Peter's in Rome, the way you round a small corner and the entire basilica is wide open in front of you. We have a good time in bed. She'll moan. I'll say "Darling, is that

passion?" She says, "No, for Christ's sake, I got this Joseph Conrad stuck in my ribs." We both have to have books in our pockets at all times. In our beds. On our walls. Right now I'm traveling with — *(He takes a paperback from his right jacket pocket, surprised.)* — Rilke! *Duino Elegies. (Opens.)* "All this was a trust and I was not up to it." Best poems written this century. *(He takes a paperback from the left jacket pocket.)* P. G. Wodehouse. *Luck of the Bodkins.*
DEIRDRE.   Hardly neglected.
SCOOPER.   All the time I have to have a book. Words on the eyeball. It must create an erotic pressure. The physical rubbing of the words against the eyeball, kneading, prodding, massaging, grazing like this sensuous cow on the green pastures of your eye. And the thought, the illumination, the comprehension! Yes, that's the orgasm. You'd love her.
DEIRDRE.   I must meet her.
SCOOPER.   I even think of Doctor James as a literary experience. Before Doctor James, my life was pages spilled all over the floor. Grim. Violent. Aimless. He's edited my life into a novel I am so proud to be a part of. Jane Austen. That kind of clarity and effervescence. And intelligence.
DEIRDRE.   Nothing's worth it if it's not a great artistic event.
SCOOPER.   She wouldn't continue with me unless I kept up the therapy. I started doing the therapy as a bouquet for her. Then the therapy turned into analysis and here we are.
DEIRDRE.   She sounds very positive.
SCOOPER.   She is so healthy. She's been going to the shrink since she was about two. She has grown up on the couch. Then our affair sent her back into therapy.
DEIRDRE.   Not Doctor James.
SCOOPER.   No! She goes to group.
DEIRDRE.   Group. Eccch.
SCOOPER.   And her husband is in another.
DEIRDRE.   She's married.
SCOOPER.   The Loch Ness Monster lives.
DEIRDRE.   Oh dear. Of course. The three children. Saint Peter's Basilica.
SCOOPER.   She was so unhappy over our affair and guilty that

her husband began to feel guilty because he didn't know about our affair and started blaming himself for her grief, so he went into therapy and he was in one group and asked her to join him in his group but she was already in another group and she wanted me to join the group her husband was in and then she'd join too, and I said I did not think that was a good idea.
DEIRDRE. I'm with you all the way there.
SCOOPER. I said I'll go to Doctor James for you, but no group analysis.
DEIRDRE. Only teaches you another kind of social chitchat.
SCOOPER. Unless it helps.
DEIRDRE. Of course. And what do your five A.M. friends say to all this?
SCOOPER. The Lispenards? It *is* the Lispenards. Valerie is one half of the Lispenards.
DEIRDRE. And the other half is —
SCOOPER. Ted. My college friend. My business partner. I suddenly see something so clearly. I get in a panic and I can't think straight. You have cleared my head. My God. I see. *(Music. Cacophony. Colors: red, purple, swirling. Henny moves blindly through the room, clutching a statue of Saint Jude. Scooper stands on the couch to get out of her way.)* That vicious rotten human being. Literally rotten.
DEIRDRE. Valerie?
SCOOPER. My mother. She did it on purpose. She knew I was leaving. That's why she waited till yesterday. This operation. This cancer caper. All designed to keep me from going. *(Henny is gone. Quiet. Lights back to normal.)* I don't know how she knew but she knew. Mystic connection.
DEIRDRE. Don't assign her magic powers.
SCOOPER. You don't think she died.
DEIRDRE. On the table?
SCOOPER. Eighty-three. Wouldn't be unheard of. Oh Christ.
DEIRDRE. Believe it or not, mastectomy is simple surgery. The breast doesn't involve any major body function like breathing or digesting.
SCOOPER. *(Takes out his cellular phone and dials.)* I'm trying to get information on the outcome of an operation? Could you connect me with — *(To Deirdre.)* They put me on hold.

DEIRDRE. She'll be all right.
SCOOPER. That breast nursed me. Fed me. My first connection. All the time I spend pursuing wombs, hidden under infinities of skirts, entry to that warm darkness, and to see what I'm searching for, hanging there. Light shining on what no light should ever shine. This fucking old lady thinks it's her bladder. If I'm conceived out of a bladder, what does that make me? Get me off hold! Operator! Operator! *(He snaps the wine glass in his hand.)* Goddamnit!!! *(Deirdre runs out of the room.)* I want the recovery room! Okay. Back on hold. If that's the way you want it. *(Deirdre returns with a basin of water and bandages. She takes his hand and washes the cut.)*
DEIRDRE. "All happy families are alike." I don't know about you but I find Tolstoy very comforting.
SCOOPER. Are you a nurse?
DEIRDRE. *(Avoiding the question.)* I hope you're not a concert pianist. Don't have to give a concert tonight.
SCOOPER. I'm an analyst.
DEIRDRE. But Doctor James —
SCOOPER. A computer analyst. Don't laugh.
DEIRDRE. I just had this mental image of all these angst-ridden computers jumping up on your couch. Help me! Help me!
SCOOPER. This customer calls me up, falling apart like the flight deck at Bellevue and he tells me his secretary wiped out a system file and now his computer screen only displays the "Blue Screen of Death." Rows of zeros and ones, an undecipherable hexadecimal code. "Calm down," I say. "We'll restore the system using the Emergency Repair Disk. Do a hard reset, run the repair option, restore the original system files, run the scan-disk utility and the operating system will come back up." And that's how I speak all day.
DEIRDRE. What does Hannah Arendt say? "Without passport and language we are nothing."
SCOOPER. Well, exactly. I love the way the light streams in your apartment.
DEIRDRE. I said once before I died, I'd finally live in a place filled with light.
SCOOPER. Heat banging its fists against the window trying to

get in. *(Into the phone.)* Operator! I'm here! Don't go away! *(But she has.)* Should I dial again?
DEIRDRE.   Hang on there.
SCOOPER.   OK. Oh God. *(He buries his face in his hands. Pause.)*
DEIRDRE.   You know who's tragically neglected? The Japanese. Kawabata.
SCOOPER.   Is he the one with the private army who disemboweled himself?
DEIRDRE.   That's Mishima.
SCOOPER.   Is Kawabata the one who has the Japanese married couple traveling to all the puppet shows in Japan? A dying art to mirror a dying marriage?
DEIRDRE.   No, that's Tanazaki.
SCOOPER.   Is Kawabata the one who writes about the whorehouse where an old man rents drugged young girls and holds them in his arms all night, never fucking them. Just holding them.
DEIRDRE.   That's Kawabata!
SCOOPER.   So that's Kawabata. So neglected.
DEIRDRE.   He won the Nobel Prize.
SCOOPER.   *(Disdainful.)* Pearl Buck won the Nobel Prize. *(Impressed.)* Now Isaac Bashevis Singer.
DEIRDRE.   I cut something out of an old *TV Guide*. "*Dick Cavett Show*. Dick's guest tonight will be the singer, Isaac Bashevis."
SCOOPER.   You have to show that to me.
DEIRDRE.   I showed it to Saul Bellow and he was sending it out for Christmas cards.
SCOOPER.   You know Saul Bellow???
DEIRDRE.   Well ...
SCOOPER.   You know someone who won the Nobel Prize???
DEIRDRE.   Oh, he's not my only Nobel Prize winner. I cradled Joseph Brodsky in my arms right over there. Derek Walcott over there. I have authors in and out of here.
SCOOPER.   *(Into the phone.)* Yes? I'm calling to see if my mother has come down from surgery yet? I know you're busy but — her name is — has she even gone into surgery? I'm not trying to sell this info to the Chinese, believe me. You advise me not to stay at

the hospital while the operation's on but then you won't — she's blind, she'll wake up and not know where — there was a brownout?
DEIRDRE.   Happened here this morning. Lights just dim.
SCOOPER.   Nobody's gone into surgery yet? When are they going into surgery? I have a plane to catch! *(He slams the phone down.)* She hasn't even gone in yet.
DEIRDRE.   You're leaving?
SCOOPER.   Five o'clock.
DEIRDRE.   Tonight?
SCOOPER.   Haiti.
DEIRDRE.   This time of year?
SCOOPER.   She's trying to stop me.
DEIRDRE.   The sidewalks are buckling and you're going to the jungle?
SCOOPER.   It's so blindingly clear.
DEIRDRE.   Don't people usually go to Haiti in the winter?
SCOOPER.   She's been saving that breast to whip out just at an instant like this. *(Cacophony. Music. Colors: green, purple. Henny gropes her way blindly through the room, waving the statue of Staint Jude.)*
DEIRDRE.   The heat in August. Frying pan. Fire.
SCOOPER.   Hiding that whammy there in her bra.
DEIRDRE.   But I suppose it's a different kind of heat.
SCOOPER.   To stop me with guilt. Stop me with caring. *(Henny is gone. Lights to normal. Quiet.)*
DEIRDRE.   But people always say a different kind of heat.
SCOOPER.   The caring is over.
DEIRDRE.   Still — hot is hot.
SCOOPER.   My heart is sealed up.
DEIRDRE.   On the other hand —
SCOOPER.   I have to keep reminding myself she is a crazy old lady crippled by fear. Two years at a window waving plastic statues of fictional saints over a bleeding breast. God, Haiti. Tropic. Lush.
DEIRDRE.   Isn't there revolution in Haiti?
SCOOPER.   Everything's in revolution! She's not stopping me. Olaffson's Hotel. Great white Victorian bric-a-brac gingerbread

hotel there in the jungle. Victorian. Voodoo. Volcanoes.
DEIRDRE.   If you need any Valium.
SCOOPER.   I'll have Valerie.
DEIRDRE.   You're taking Valerie?
SCOOPER.   Our first trip together. Finally. The decision.
DEIRDRE.   What does her husband say to all this?
SCOOPER.   We haven't told him yet. We've left a letter for him at his group tonight. We felt that was the kindest thing to do. He goes right from work to group. He couldn't read a letter like the one we've left him alone. He's so dependent on his group. Poor, weak … don't get me started on Ted.
DEIRDRE.   Should be an interesting session.
SCOOPER.   In a way I'd like to be there. What was Hemingway's phrase? Grace under pressure? I don't think Ted Lispenard will personify grace under pressure.
DEIRDRE.   And you'll be in Haiti.
SCOOPER.   Four weeks.
DEIRDRE.   The time Doctor James is away.
SCOOPER.   Her sister will take the kids. When we get back we'll start looking for a place in Maine. Get out of this neurotic city. Find a beat-up ramshackle house by the sea. Remodel it. Books. Music. Comfort. Valerie says she wants a house like us. Simple on the outside. But inside. Inside! We have this dream of buying up every book in Maine.
DEIRDRE.   That shouldn't be hard.
SCOOPER.   Open the world's greatest bookstore. Publish newsletters written by people telling what books they love. A bookstore open twenty-four hours a day. 800 numbers! Web sites!
DEIRDRE.   Like L.L. Bean.
SCOOPER.   Yes! People will flock to us from all over the world and we'll grow and grow until one day the entire town is one bookstore.
DEIRDRE.   The elephant graveyard.
SCOOPER.   A Vatican of books. "If we don't have it, they didn't write it."
DEIRDRE.   You'll finish your treatment?
SCOOPER.   Finishing my treatment is not the most important thing in the world. I'm almost finished with Doctor James any-

way. Except for this one dream I have that even the great dream-decipherer himself can't figure out.
DEIRDRE.   Please? I might be able to help —
SCOOPER.   I am this little boy. All dressed up.
DEIRDRE.   New clothes. Masquerade.
SCOOPER.   A strange city.
DEIRDRE.   Outsider. Go on.
SCOOPER.   Facing a strange man.
DEIRDRE.   And you're a small child. And it's not your father. Hmmm.
SCOOPER.   And my mother who is all dolled up —
DEIRDRE.   A new beginning?
SCOOPER.   Picks me up and begins hitting this man with me.
DEIRDRE.   Using you as a weapon?
SCOOPER.   And she's screaming, "You neglected me! You neglected me!"
DEIRDRE.   And then you wake up?
SCOOPER.   It's so alive in my mind.
DEIRDRE.   I could figure that out.
SCOOPER.   I really wish you wouldn't.
DEIRDRE.   Strange city. Outsider. A dream of betrayal.
SCOOPER.   I didn't say betrayal. I said neglect.
DEIRDRE.   Neglect is always betrayal.
SCOOPER.   Is that a quote?
DEIRDRE.   That's a belief.
SCOOPER.   If he can't figure it out — talk about *Pride and Prejudice* — I don't think you can. Stay out of it. OK?
DEIRDRE.   I'll butt out of your head. Fine.
SCOOPER.   But I know the key to everything is in that dream.
DEIRDRE.   Oh, I see! If you solve the dream, you'll have to leave him.
SCOOPER.   I want to leave him!
DEIRDRE.   I didn't say you didn't.
SCOOPER.   He's getting a postcard from me with a volcano on it and the message reads "Doctor, see this volcano? This is me" ... Suppose she's dead. Suppose she died? *(He takes out the phone and rapidly punches in the numbers. Waits. Then:)* New York-Presbyterian — is this — ? What number have I — ? *(He puts*

the phone down in agony, then works his face into a big smile. He lifts the phone again.) Ted! Hi! What are you doing home? No, my fingers were just dialing. And I dialed. Summer cold? Oh no. They're the worst. Go back to sleep. You shouldn't answer the phone if you're sick. Are you going to Group tonight? No, you mustn't miss that. Take care. Oh. Valerie called? What time did she leave for New Hampshire? Great. Listen, thank you for the flowers. She was barely in the hospital when the flowers arrived. Really sweet. I don't know yet. But the best doctors. Thank you. Yes. Yes. Very dear of you. No! Yes. I'll tell her. Thank you. Yes. Of course! Yes. Yes. She will. Yes. Yes. Fine. Yes. Could you do me a favor? Valerie wanted a report on how my mother is. I'm not at home. Could you have Valerie call my cellular? Absolutely. All the best. Take care. Yes. Yes. *(He hangs up. He is furious.)* Asshole! You don't send flowers to a blind person. You treat her senses. You send candy. That's Ted in a nutshell. Oh, fuck. This atmosphere of lying. Every day for the past five years, living life with this Pavlovian smile trapped on my face. Inside I'm dying. *(Deirdre looks at him with disdain.)*
DEIRDRE. Betraying your five A.M. friends.
SCOOPER. It didn't seem like betraying. The love sweetened everything.
DEIRDRE. You mean it poisoned everything. Like the silence of your mother's sickness.
SCOOPER. *(Reaching for a book.)* Joseph Conrad. *Chance*! This is one of the books stuck in Valerie's ribs.
DEIRDRE. *(Disillusioned.)* One of the great neglected masterpieces.
SCOOPER. I love this damned book.
DEIRDRE. So did I.
SCOOPER. "Life demands a man and a woman." *(He searches through the book.)*
DEIRDRE. Page 432. "Pairing off is the fate of mankind."
SCOOPER. *(Reading.)* "If two beings thrown together, mutually attract ... voluntarily stop short of the — the embrace —"
DEIRDRE. *(Quoting.)* ... "they are committing a sin against life. The call of which is simple."
BOTH. "Perhaps sacred." *(A pause. They look at each other.*

They're very close. They start to kiss.)
SCOOPER. *(Softly.)* It's taken Valerie and me five years to get to this day. I don't want to get mixed up with another married lady.
DEIRDRE. I'm not married.
SCOOPER. Raymond.
DEIRDRE. There is no Raymond. I only told you that — a girl has to be — a woman has to be — I call myself a woman when I'm working, but when I'm alone in this apartment, I'm a girl. A girl has to be careful. I don't know you. A patient. I don't know what you're seeing him for. You might be a psychopath. I wanted you to think someone was coming home.
SCOOPER. You wear a wedding ring.
DEIRDRE. A friend advised me to. It avoids hassles.
SCOOPER. A close friend?
DEIRDRE. *(Pulls away.)* What time is your plane?
SCOOPER. Five o'clock.
DEIRDRE. Busy day. Very active. Very healthy. Haiti. *Comedians.*
SCOOPER. I don't know who's playing down there.
DEIRDRE. Graham Greene. Novel. Haiti. In this pile.
SCOOPER. I've never read that.
DEIRDRE. I'd like to give it to you.
SCOOPER. Sign it?
DEIRDRE. *(Digging angrily in the stacks.)* Where the fuck is it? Here. In the Evelyn Waugh pile. That's neglected. When one author ends up in another author's pile.
SCOOPER. They're all English. Easy mistake.
DEIRDRE. Your hand is all right?
SCOOPER. All fine.
DEIRDRE. *(Writing in the book.)* "Be careful in the jungle."
SCOOPER. You sound like my mother.
DEIRDRE. Why did you pick me up today?
SCOOPER. I told you. The breeze around your legs —
DEIRDRE. We shared the same waiting room for so many months in silence. I spend so many sessions asking Doctor James, Why isn't that man looking at me? I even got it into my head that Doctor James had hired you to drive me mad, to

ignore me, to come for your session even before my session.
SCOOPER. I came to prepare. I calm myself. A quiet place to read.
DEIRDRE. You'd loom outside that door. I'd be inside on the couch. You'd be out there, doing God knows what. Listening at the door. Laughing at me.
SCOOPER. Never. I was reading.
DEIRDRE. I begged Doctor James to change appointments. Please! I don't want to be annihilated by that man.
SCOOPER. And he only said Why does the presence of that man annoy you?
DEIRDRE. You were listening.
SCOOPER. How could I hear with his air conditioner on?
DEIRDRE. You became my father. My lovers. My teachers. My uncles. My bosses. Every man who's ever gone out of this way to ignore me. I found myself dressing for you. Would he notice this? I'll show him. I would stand up naked in this window and wait for you to come out of your appointment. I'd do hypnotism things. Now he'll look up. Now he'll see me.
SCOOPER. I was deep in my own problems.
DEIRDRE. So you missed my breakdown.
SCOOPER. When was it?
DEIRDRE. Last October.
SCOOPER. Last October. That was a rough time for me last October.
DEIRDRE. I had one of the world's greatest uninstitutionalized breakdowns with weeping and moaning and Doctor James pulling magic tricks out of the air to keep me out of a hospital and you sit there turning the pages.
SCOOPER. I was reading Herman Melville. *Pierre*. His last novel. His most misunderstood —
DEIRDRE. You ignore me for eleven months and today you are suddenly obsessed with unculminated desire to pick me up.
SCOOPER. *Pierre* is Melville's only novel that takes place on land. You're an attractive woman.
DEIRDRE. I have been for the last eleven months. It's still the same flesh.
SCOOPER. Edith Wharton says beauty is the genius of the skin.

DEIRDRE. Did Doctor James say "Take her. She's lonely. She's mad. She's out roaming the streets right now. My going-away present from doctor to patient. I can't mess around with her because of the Hippocratic oath, but you give her a good boff for me." Is that what the mind butcher said to you? Is that how you spend your sessions? Talking about me? How many other patients has old stud Doctor James fixed you up with? The mother who drinks? Is she another one of your old discards? You are wasting your $140 an hour. The two of you. Two Freudian mind fuckers. He tells you all my secrets? The two of you having a bloody good laugh on my account? I thought you and I shared Doctor James. Brothers and sisters? Going in to visit our father? Brothers and sisters? Hah!
SCOOPER. One hundred forty dollars an hour?
DEIRDRE. I suddenly understand incest.
SCOOPER. One hundred forty dollars an hour???
DEIRDRE. You have successfully ruined Doctor James for his analysand. I can never go back to him again.
SCOOPER. He charges me $150 an hour.
DEIRDRE. $150 an hour?
SCOOPER. He charges you $140 an hour?
DEIRDRE. $140.
SCOOPER. Why does he charge me $150?
DEIRDRE. He charges you $150?
SCOOPER. 150 and 140? It doesn't seem fair.
DEIRDRE. He charges me 140 because I am his favorite patient.
SCOOPER. Don't say that.
DEIRDRE. Sometimes he doesn't even charge me. Sometimes he says you are so interesting, I should be giving you money just for the privilege of listening to you pour out your heart.
SCOOPER. He doesn't say that.
DEIRDRE. No, he doesn't.
SCOOPER. But he does charge you 140.
DEIRDRE. 140.
SCOOPER. How many days a week?
DEIRDRE. Five.
SCOOPER. How many years?

DEIRDRE. Eight.
SCOOPER. You must be very sick.
DEIRDRE. How long for you?
SCOOPER. Six.
DEIRDRE. How many days a week?
SCOOPER. The three I see you.
DEIRDRE. Oh, therapy. You're only in therapy.
SCOOPER. I'm in analysis.
DEIRDRE. Three days a week? Gerber's Baby Food analysis. On the other hand, we have me! Five days a week! Depths of my psyche! Sonar waves into my soul! Psychic barium cocktails.
SCOOPER. Wait. You go early in the morning.
DEIRDRE. Gallop straight from my dreams to the couch.
SCOOPER. Oh, I know what you're in.
DEIRDRE. Doctor can't wait to start off his day with a high.
SCOOPER You're in supportive analysis.
DEIRDRE. Deep classical.
SCOOPER. You're one of those sad neurotics who have to go first thing in the morning just to get enough courage —
DEIRDRE. What Beethoven is to the sonata, I am to the couch!
SCOOPER. — just to get through the day.
DEIRDRE. I am not in supportive.
SCOOPER. You're one of those cripples who can only take life in twenty-four-hour doses. Then off to Daddy.
DEIRDRE. I am very strong.
SCOOPER. When did he say you were strong?
DEIRDRE. You're the one who listens at the door. You tell me.
SCOOPER. He hardly says anything ever to me.
DEIRDRE. To me he gives wonders.
SCOOPER. All I know is I possess enough strength to get through a simple day.
DEIRDRE. To me he tells secrets of living.
SCOOPER. I only need him three days a week.
DEIRDRE. He reads to me from the Secret Freud Handbook.
SCOOPER. I don't use him for a crutch.
DEIRDRE. He wants me to be free.
SCOOPER. I don't think Doctor James likes the kind of patient who uses him for a crutch.

DEIRDRE.　He says Deirdre, I learn from you!
SCOOPER.　He has you first just to get the worst out of the way.
DEIRDRE.　It boils down to this.
SCOOPER.　He's not helping you if he's charging you charity fees.
DEIRDRE.　I am in analysis. You are in therapy. You are going to him for one specific problem. Your girlfriend. Your mother. I am going to him for my whole life. All the fantasies I wasted on you. I had you trapped in this Dostoevskian turmoil. A fellow tormentee. Someone who is my match. Someone who understands. What do I get picked up by? Cuticle despair. Is that why the little baby's going to Doctor James? His little cuticle hurts?
SCOOPER.　You're being very hostile.
DEIRDRE.　You have discovered the mouth of the River Hostility. You are drowning in the Great Lakes of Hostility.
SCOOPER.　Don't say that.
DEIRDRE.　Oh, little baby can dish it out. But little baby can't take it. You want to know why I'm spending the best years of my life on Doctor James' couch? And it looks like my sunset years. You want to know the magic event that will clarify everything for you? Little magic key revelations? I hurt someone. Hurt them very badly.
SCOOPER.　You don't mean breaking hearts.
DEIRDRE.　We both share a relationship of a long nature with a married person. *(She lights a cigarette.)*
SCOOPER.　Of which sex?
DEIRDRE.　A married person. This married person sat in a hotel room and told me this person was going back to their mate. Finally. Over. I had trouble hearing because the ashtray on the table between us started talking to me. The ashtray was empty because both of us had stopped smoking. We had met at a SmokEnders clinic and it made us think we had a great deal in common and we had both not smoked for a long time now and I felt proud of that. But now words like "Over" and "Returning" became our vocabularies' main themes and this ashtray says to me Just because you don't smoke anymore doesn't mean you have to neglect me. And the ashtray starts singing in this

lovely clear voice the old Jerome Kern standard "Why Was I Born?" And this person whose lungs I have helped clear packs a suitcase and calls room service and orders a pack of cigarettes. Camels. Lucky Strikes. Anything without a filter. And I knew it was over. And we sat there a long time. Room service brings the smokes. A pot of decaffeinated coffee. And the ashtray suddenly stops singing and says I'll tell you why you were born. To free yourself. Do it. Use me! I picked up the ashtray and could see the person all distorted in its glass base. I brought it down on the side of the person's head.

SCOOPER. Did you kill this person?

DEIRDRE. The person turned to light the cigarette. The match flew out of my friend's hand and landed on blue pajamas which I thought were silk but were this incendiary Orlon and the suitcase burst into flame and I threw the decaf coffee on the bed and put out the fire and called room service to take care of this person with the gash on the person's head and in a secret way found Doctor James and have been going to him every day since that day.

SCOOPER. This person. Was it a man or a woman?

DEIRDRE. It was a man, goddamnit. *(She raises the ashtray over him with great violence.)* A man! You're like every other man I ever met in my life. You come on like this great oral aggressive, but at heart you're this anal retentive ...

SCOOPER. I think ... I really wish you would put that down. I'm not like your friend. I stopped smoking and have not started up. Put it down. *(She puts the ashtray down quietly and slumps to the floor in agony.)* I saw you in the waiting room. I couldn't look at you because of the desperation smeared all over your face. I said Is that what I look like?

DEIRDRE. Then you must have felt some sympathy for me. If you saw my agony.

SCOOPER. There's no sympathy in a doctor's waiting room. Only me next! Me next! I picked you up today because I was sad Doctor James was leaving, crazy because I am finally leaving with the woman I love after a trillion years of waiting. I'm losing a close friend, Ted, my old college roommate. And my mother's body bursts open and I'm furious at her for not trust-

ing me enough to tell me two years ago and I see you, beside the books, and I just wanted to connect to you.
DEIRDRE.   E. M. Forster says that. Connect. Only connect.
SCOOPER.   Fuck E. M. Forster. I just wanted to sit down and share.
DEIRDRE.   And what did you find out?
SCOOPER.   That I'm being overcharged.
DEIRDRE.   I'm sorry I said you were only in therapy.
SCOOPER.   It's the meanest thing anybody ever said to me.
DEIRDRE.   Well, if that's the meanest thing —
SCOOPER.   I'd better go. Up to the hospital. Find out what I can before I'm off. *(He picks up his suitcase and stands at the door.)* We'll meet again.
DEIRDRE.   You'll be all healthy, living with the world's most perfect woman. I don't think we'll meet.
SCOOPER.   Thank you for the Greene. *(He goes. Silence.)*
DEIRDRE.   *(Calls out.)* My father lives in New Jersey.
SCOOPER.   *(Returning.)* Recuperating from his death in the Lake Placid car crash?
DEIRDRE.   He lives in a nursing home. Which is why I asked you before if your mother was in a nursing home. If I can help in any way. We both share a guilt about the way we neglected a parent.
SCOOPER.   I haven't neglected anybody ...
DEIRDRE.   It's a very good nursing home. It's a lot but the Medicare helps out. My father was in the Mafia. You don't have to be Italian to be in the Mafia. He was in charge of all the pinball machines in the state of New Jersey. Atlantic City. Up through the Jersey Shore. I didn't mind that. But when I was twenty, I found out that he had gone over to drugs and was pushing drugs. Fairly large quantities in the same areas where he previously had had the pinballs . . I found that out inadvertently. He kept things from me. Loved that I read and was smart. But when I found out about the drugs. Heroin. Did I tell you it was heroin? I blew the whistle on him. I called the FBI. They arrested him. It was on the front pages of lots of papers. Daughter Turns in Father. Do you remember me? Sometimes for a while after that, people would recognize my face. I wrote

a book about it.
SCOOPER. *(In awe.)* You wrote one of these?
DEIRDRE. Long before the day of the big paperback sale. Still I got an advance you'd call tidy. *Turn-In: The Story of a Daughter.*
SCOOPER. I don't know it.
DEIRDRE. Talk about neglected. It never took off the way they hoped. Out of print. No copies. The FBI gave me a new identity. After I named names and after I named Papa, our family no longer existed. I no longer had the right to use my family name.
SCOOPER. Deirdre is not your name?
DEIRDRE. No, that's all I kept. Deirdre I kept. But this hair ... this face ... this body, all new.
SCOOPER. All new?
DEIRDRE. The FBI set me up here. Helped me get started.
SCOOPER. This is a government bookstore?
DEIRDRE. No. Then they left me on my own. All I had was my books.
SCOOPER. Do you miss your old life? My God, losing everything. You're quite beautiful now. They did ... whoever, a wonderful job.
DEIRDRE. Do I miss my old life? No, strangely, what I miss ... the moment I can't lose is the moment I turned my father in. The moment I called.
SCOOPER. You can't do that too often.
DEIRDRE. I know, and now that he's not available, I do the next best thing.
SCOOPER. Which is?
DEIRDRE. I call up the spouses of authors who mean the world to me.
SCOOPER. And say what?
DEIRDRE. Look up Norman Mailer. I know how to sow the seeds. *(Scooper looks through the Rolodex.)*
SCOOPER. You don't have a computer. I could set you up in a second.
DEIRDRE. My concessions to the future stop with the Rolodex.
SCOOPER. That is so admirable. My God, the names here — Saul Bellow. William Styron.

DEIRDRE. Dial Norman Mailer.
SCOOPER. Brooklyn. 718 area code. *(Scooper punches the numbers.)* It's ringing.
DEIRDRE. *(Takes the phone.)* Mrs. Mailer? Mrs. Norman Mailer? Yes. Could you please give Norman — I mean Mr. Mailer — a message? Tell him it's Deirdre calling. Tell him his book is ready. Tell him his special order is ready. The special order. The one he was dying for. *(She hangs up.)*
SCOOPER. But you could get him in trouble.
DEIRDRE. Why do you think he's been married so many times?
SCOOPER. You are incredible. Do another one.
DEIRDRE. Spin the Rolodex!
SCOOPER. Doctorow, E. L.
DEIRDRE. Dial!
SCOOPER. *(Dials.)* It's a machine.
DEIRDRE. *(Takes the phone.)* Edgar. It's Deirdre waiting for you again and again and again, Edgar, we can repeat the past. Yes. Yes. Yes. *(She hangs up.)*
SCOOPER. I want to try one! *(Scooper finds a name and dials.)* May I speak to Joan Didion? Is this her husband? Yes, Mr. Dunne, I'd like to leave a message. Tell her it's ... Tell her it's Herman Melville and I want to hear Joan cry out *"Omoo"* once more. I want to hear her cry out *"Typee."* Do you have that? *"Omoo! Typee!"* *(He hangs up.)* Holy Christ, this is fantastic! I want to call Susan Sontag!
DEIRDRE. *(Takes phone from him.)* My father was in the Big House for a long time.
SCOOPER. Is he still in the Big House?
DEIRDRE. He's out now. He developed this very bad arthritis in prison. And his stomach is gone from taking so many aspirins for his arthritis. I'm hoping one day before he dies we can clear the books. He will lean over and take my hand and say I understand why you did what you did. So I go out there every weekend, sit there, read. Out loud. Wait for the scene. That moment that will clarify all. I've gone through James Joyce and Wallace Stevens.
SCOOPER. Does a Mafia Chief understand it?

DEIRDRE. I don't know. I only hope he'll hear the voice underneath. English has the largest vocabulary of any language and perhaps one day I'll come up with the right combination and my father will forgive me for putting him away for ten years in the slammer.
SCOOPER. You put a lot of faith in the language.
DEIRDRE. Yes. Yes, I do. *(They embrace, hungrily.)*
SCOOPER. What you've been through. I'd like to show you how much I care for you.
DEIRDRE. *(Undoes his tie.)* Care for Dr. James. Care for our work.
SCOOPER. What are you reading to your father now?
DEIRDRE. *(Unbuttons his collar button.)* The South Americans.
SCOOPER. *(Pulls the tie off his shirt.)* Don't get me started on the South Americans.
DEIRDRE. Jorge Amado. *(She closes the curtains. Darkness. She turns on a light over the bed.)*
SCOOPER. *(Undressing as fast as he can.)* The Two Loves of Dona Flor. *(Deirdre opens the cabinets under a shelf of books and pulls out a bed.)*
DEIRDRE. Gabriella Clove and Cinnamon.
SCOOPER. *(Takes off his trousers.)* A Hundred Years of Solitude.
DEIRDRE. *(Steps out of the other shoe.)* Marquez is hardly neglected.
SCOOPER. *(Kicks off a shoe.)* A cult book.
DEIRDRE. *(Unbuttons her blouse.)* But not neglected. Overpraised.
SCOOPER. *(Unbuttons his shirt.)* But perfect.
DEIRDRE. *(Undoing her skirt.)* Of its kind. But like all cult books ultimately overpraised. *(They get into bed.)*
SCOOPER. Think of me as an eclipse.
DEIRDRE. An eclipse?
SCOOPER. Let me move into your orbit. Let me blot out the vision of your father. Oh God, you poor girl, what you've been through. I'd like to show you how much I care for you —
DEIRDRE. Care for Doctor James, care for our work —
SCOOPER. Care for our meeting —
DEIRDRE. Have you ever been to South America?
SCOOPER. No. No. But emotionally I identify with the South

Americans.

DEIRDRE. I'd like to put another woman's body between you and the image of that half-rotten peach. That poisoned gauze. Restore the womb to its proper dark place. Do you read Valéry?

SCOOPER. Do I read to Valerie?

DEIRDRE. Paul Valéry.

SCOOPER. I don't read French.

DEIRDRE. I don't either.

SCOOPER. Your first edition of Byron.

DEIRDRE. Shall we read it?

SCOOPER. It's uncut. *(She takes a paper knife.)* It'll reduce the value. I'll cut just one page. *(He takes the paper knife from her. He takes one of the Byron volumes. He slices the page, opens the book and carefully reads:)* "But some are dead and some are gone And some are scattered and alone And some are rebels on the hills ..." *(He gives her the book and the knife. She slices open a page and reads.)*

DEIRDRE. He says, "Had Orpheus fiddled at the present hour He'd see lions waltzing in the tower."

SCOOPER. The pressure.

DEIRDRE. The sound.

SCOOPER. The pages resist.

DEIRDRE. Gentle. *(She cuts another page.)*

SCOOPER. Feels good. *(He cuts another page.)*

DEIRDRE. Firm. *(She cuts another page.)*

SCOOPER. Slice. *(He cuts another page.)*

DEIRDRE. The odor.

SCOOPER. The feel.

DEIRDRE. The paper.

SCOOPER. The binding.

DEIRDRE. The print.

SCOOPER. The ink.

DEIRDRE. So neglected.

SCOOPER. So neglected. *(They each cut a page. They drop the books. They embrace hungrily. He turns off the light. Dark. Laughter. Passion. The phone rings. It rings.)*

DEIRDRE. No.

SCOOPER. Hospital hospital hospital — *(Picks up the phone.)*

Yes? Valerie! *(Deirdre turns on the light. Scooper is naked.)* How was New Hampshire? *(He signals Deirdre to turn off that light. Darkness again.)* I'm just at a friend's house. The operation — I don't know — there was a brownout. Chicken pox? What are you talking about. She has cancer. Bradley has chicken pox? *(He turns on the light. He has his shorts on. Deirdre now lies on the couch, the bedspread wrapped around her, her arms over her eyes.)* They turned you back from the camp? Sophie might have chicken pox? Kim might have it? They're all home with you? You drove all the way up to New Hampshire with them and now they're all back with you? Can't your sister— *(He turns the light off. Blackness.)* It's very difficult to talk right now. Why didn't you give him shots? You have no right to say that — what are you saying? Our affair took up so much time that you have neglected your kids? Stop crying. *(He turns the light back on. He now has his shirt on. Deirdre goes out of the room.)* Chicken pox is not dangerous. You are not a terrible woman. I don't care if you've never had chicken pox. I've never had chicken pox. We can still get on the plane. We'll start a worldwide epidemic of chicken pox. I don't care. I want us to be off. Don't cry, Val! Val! Valerie! Hi, Ted. Listen, Ted, we might as well cut the shit — Valerie is not unpacking from New Hampshire. Those bags are for me. She is packing for me. Ted, you might as well know. Valerie and I are going to Haiti tonight. When you get to your group, you'll find a letter from us. Ted, Valerie and I — Val, get off the extension. Let me tell him! Valerie, I'll be right over there to pick you up. Ted, we have been screwing right under your nose for the past five years. Valerie, put that phone down. Valerie, it's the only time we can go. With the doctor. I've met a wonderful person who'll help us with our books. Valerie? I'll be right over. Ted. Put Valerie on. Hello? *(He hangs up. Deirdre returns wearing a bathrobe. Pause.)* Her kid's got chicken pox.
DEIRDRE. *(So pleased.)* Oh. I'm sorry.
SCOOPER. Psychosomatic chicken pox.
DEIRDRE. What a month we can have! New York in August! You can get into any restaurant. Movies are empty and cool! Movies! We'll see every movie in town and get icicles on us from watching — should we see only films adapted from books and

sit in the theater with flashlights and read along with the movie? Day trips to the beach! Museums! *(She opens the curtains. Light streams in.)* Look! The pianist comes out. Is he weeping? No, the pianist is dancing! He is healed! *(She puts on a CD: joyous Bach.*)* When you said you were reading Rilke, I couldn't believe it. I fell in love with you at that moment. I can mark my love.

SCOOPER. I just picked up Rilke. I'm not familiar with Rilke.

DEIRDRE. We have been given a gift!

SCOOPER. She didn't leave him.

DEIRDRE. One day you will write that lady such a thank you note!

SCOOPER. She promised she'd leave him.

DEIRDRE. And people make promises and people break promises —

SCOOPER. You know what I blame it all on?

DEIRDRE. Don't blame it on anybody. To be our ages and unattached.

SCOOPER. I never read a book that had a thing to do with my life. *(Scooper stacks books in a pile as tall as he is.)*

DEIRDRE. Don't you hear me? *(She turns off the music.)*

SCOOPER. We're the subsidiary characters in everybody's lives. That's the joke, the joke of our lives. We spend all our time babbling to Herr Doktor across the street about ourselves and we don't figure in anyone's life. I bring my life to Doctor James and we turn my life into a lullaby until I am as fictional to myself as any one of these books are to me. *(He stands back to study the stack of books. He leaps forward and assaults the stack. He begins ripping the books.)* I wish I were blind! And illiterate! I wish I could rip all the sight out of my head. *(He destroys one book, then another.)* Were you a nun? Were you an orphan! Is your father in the Mafia! Are you even in books!

DEIRDRE. *(Throws herself on the books.)* Don't rip my books! Stop it! *(Scooper pushes her against a bookcase, which falls forward. Books spill out into the room.)* My ankle!

SCOOPER. *(He destroys more books.)* I want to get all this fiction out of my eyes! *(Deirdre picks up the paper knife. She stabs him. He*

---

* See Special Note on Songs and Recordings on copyright page.

is in such a fury he doesn't even feel it.) Throw them all out the window! *(Scooper starts to heave the books through the window. His shirt is covered with blood. Deirdre is limping and hysterical. Scooper stops.)* There's Doctor James. Coming out of his office.
DEIRDRE. *(Hopping to the window.)* Who's driving the blue Mercedes?
SCOOPER. A woman.
DEIRDRE. Three children.
SCOOPER. They put the luggage in the trunk.
DEIRDRE. He kisses them all.
SCOOPER. He gets in the driver's seat.
DEIRDRE. They drive away.
SCOOPER. Come back.
DEIRDRE. Come back!
SCOOPER. Doctor James, come back!
DEIRDRE. Doctor James, come back! *(They press against the glass.)*
SCOOPER. I see the car.
DEIRDRE. Turning onto Park.
SCOOPER. Doctor James.
DEIRDRE. He's gone.
SCOOPER. Doctor James.
DEIRDRE. He's gone. *(They punch each other. They stab each other. They weep and hit and attack each other. They stop. They gasp for breath.)*
SCOOPER. Put down that paper knife. I'm bleeding.
DEIRDRE. Oh dear Christ. I stabbed you. I tried to kill you.
SCOOPER. I ruined your apartment. I tried to kill you!
DEIRDRE. What's the last eight years been for? Are you dying? Are you bleeding?
SCOOPER. Is it all for naught? The last six years? All for naught?
DEIRDRE. The last eight years? All for zero? Have to get out to my father. To read to him.
SCOOPER. It can't be. Back to go. The mother.
DEIRDRE. Back to zero. The father. *(Henny appears, clutching her statue of Saint Jude. Scooper looks up at her.)*

CURTAIN

ACT TWO

A hospital room. Henny sits up in bed. It's two days after the operation. Her IV has been disconnected. In spite of her bandaging, it's the first time she's felt comfortable in years. Scooper is a patient in the hospital. He has a bathrobe on over pajamas. His side is bandaged. He sits in a wheelchair.

SCOOPER.   Ma, I'm having a lot of trouble relating to people.
HENNY.   Every time I call you, you're reading a book. And they're these books no one ever heard of.
SCOOPER.   I'm having trouble with women.
HENNY.   Don't you ever read anything by a writer who's alive?
SCOOPER.   And you are the key woman in my life. The first woman.
HENNY.   Writers write books and then they go on promotion tours on the radio and TV and a person like myself who can't read can at least hear about the person who did the writing.
SCOOPER.   I would like to examine in this time we have —
HENNY.   But you don't read them unless they sold two copies and been dead nine hundred years and nobody ever made a movie out of it or heard of it.
SCOOPER.   This relationship in a way, a manner, that might shed light on future relationships with —
HENNY.   My friend, Roberta Schildhauer, has always got her nose in a book. She wore out her library card. They had to laminate it, and she never heard of any of the stuff you read. *(Scooper holds his side by his spleen. He makes a sudden retching noise, but then is quiet.)* Is that you?
SCOOPER.   I got a crick in my side. *(He gets out of the wheelchair.)*
HENNY.   Why did the nurse come and say "Get back in bed."
SCOOPER.   There's other people in the room. She was talking to them.
HENNY.   It sounded like she was talking to you.
SCOOPER.   Get back to bed? She was being sexy.

HENNY. What does the nurse look like?
SCOOPER. She's the shortest nurse you ever saw with this great white cap on her head. It looks like this seagull has made this rest stop on her head on his way out to the horizon.
HENNY. What do you have on?
SCOOPER. Blue striped seersucker suit. Blue shirt. Blue tie with red apples on it for the Big Apple.
HENNY. You must look nice. No wonder she's being sexy. I'll get special attention if the nurses know I got a sexy son.
SCOOPER. Henny, you've been lying to me, to yourself for the past two years. You're going home in ten or twelve days. I want to make sure you won't ever lie —
HENNY. I wasn't lying —
SCOOPER. You were sick for two years and couldn't trust me. I called you most every day and saw you at Christmas and on your birthday and in all that time you acted like you were sneaking a thermos of martinis onto the beach for Daddy to drink.
HENNY. I was going to tell you —
SCOOPER. Tell me what?
HENNY. *(Sharply.)* Tell you I was frightened. What do you think?
SCOOPER. And you couldn't.
HENNY. I couldn't give you my problems.
SCOOPER. You didn't trust me?
HENNY. I was going to call the priest one day and have him come to the house and confess about the sore down there.
SCOOPER. Sores are not sins. Something in you said I do not trust this man who is my son.
HENNY. Did you put the double lock on my apartment? I don't want those people next door raiding my apartment. Oh, the old witch is finally gone. Let's get the furniture. Let's get the dishes. Wheel out the piano.
SCOOPER. Nobody wants anything in that apartment.
HENNY. You do. I'm leaving things for you. I'm collecting sheets for you. I send the girl to open bank accounts and get electric blankets and electric kettles so when you finally get married you'll be all set. You're the only boy on the block with

a hope chest.
SCOOPER. I'm not a boy, Henny. I'm thirty-eight-years-old.
HENNY. Thirty-eight? Old? You know what old is? When you look back and say Christ, to be seventy-nine again. Nostalgia for eighty. Even eighty-one. That wasn't so bad. To be that young. To be handsome.
SCOOPER. You haven't seen me in years. You don't even know what I look like.
HENNY. You look like Robert Redford.
SCOOPER. You don't know what Robert Redford looks like.
HENNY. He looks like you.
SCOOPER. Henny —
HENNY. The lucky part is I don't know what I look like either.
SCOOPER. The lucky part is this operation —
HENNY. *(Holds her ears.)* Don't talk about the operation!
SCOOPER. It was a success.
HENNY. What was a success?
SCOOPER. They got it. You're OK.
HENNY. Between my legs?
SCOOPER. They put a pessary.
HENNY. They put a pet between my legs?
SCOOPER. A silver disc to hold the uterus.
HENNY. My bladder! —
SCOOPER. You don't know. You make everything up for yourself.
HENNY. *(Reaches out her hands.)* I can drink water? It won't burn? I want water. *(Scooper gives her the pitcher. She takes it and drinks right out of the pitcher. She falls back.)*
SCOOPER. The irony is you're probably in the best health you've ever been in in your life. They said for all the neglect, you had the body of a fifty-two-year-old woman.
HENNY. Well, if they find a fifty-two-year-old soul stuck in a six-thousand-year-old body, we can do a complete switch.
SCOOPER. The good thing about being old —
HENNY. Twenty-five thousand words or less please.
SCOOPER. The cancer moves slow.
HENNY. Stop harping that word!
SCOOPER. They got it. It's out of you. Hallelujah, Saint Jude.

47

Maybe Kotex and Saint Jude are the secret of life. The disease in Fort Bosom is captured. I don't want you leaving this hospital galloping pronto back to the old evasions. Doing anything to avoid hitting center. Not lying. Just evading. I'm talking to myself as well as you. If you're in trouble, you have to tell me.
HENNY. How hot is it in this room? I'm burning up.
SCOOPER. The thermometer here on the window. Eighty-nine degrees.
HENNY. A miracle. An age I haven't been. Pick a number. Any number. I've been it. Who cares how hot it is. I'm in hell and isn't hell supposed to be hot?
SCOOPER. You got yourself in hell all by yourself.
HENNY. And I'll get myself out all by myself.
SCOOPER. Did you show your breast to me —
HENNY. Bosom!
SCOOPER. To stop me from going? I have to know this.
HENNY. Where are you going?
SCOOPER. I was only going away for a few weeks.
HENNY. You going on a trip?
SCOOPER. You had it hidden for two years. Why did you have to pick that time —
HENNY. You can't leave.
SCOOPER. I canceled the trip. Did you know?
HENNY. I'm sorry such a minor thing as this bosom incident has fouled up your summer plans.
SCOOPER. Cut the dramatics.
HENNY. I'm eighty-three. I won't be around much longer to screw up your summer vacations. If you write a piece on "My Summer Vacation," don't forget to send me a copy. I'm learning Braille with my ass. I'll sit on it and learn all I need to know.
SCOOPER. Did you show me your breast to stop me from going?
HENNY. I hate that word. Breast-beating. Why do you have to use that word — breast? Sounds like something a chicken has. I always loved my bosoms. Your father loved my bosoms. Bosom buddies. Bosoms are fun. Bosoms are round. I may not have had good legs, or had the straightest teeth, but did my bosoms get attention at the beach. I couldn't wait for summer. I'm a

topless dancer now. Half a topless dancer.
SCOOPER.   Did you know I was going away?
HENNY.   Where are you going? I don't keep track of your life. Who'd tell me?
SCOOPER.   Val. Did she let anything slip?
HENNY.   I never talk to Valerie.
SCOOPER.   She let something slip about a trip?
HENNY.   She and Ted sent flowers.
SCOOPER.   That we were going away?
HENNY.   I wish they sent candy instead. I could eat that bouquet. The food I'll tell you is not so hot here. But don't have them come visit me. They're good friends to you, but I don't want anybody up here seeing me.
SCOOPER.   Believe me, they won't be coming.
HENNY.   I wish Jack were here. Where is my Jack?
SCOOPER.   So you could kill him again?
HENNY.   Your father died because he drank and he was drunk all the time and then he drank even more and then he died.
SCOOPER.   So why do you wish such a drunk here by your side?
HENNY.   To have a man with me.
SCOOPER.   You have me.
HENNY.   Like I was saying. Where are those nurses? What do you think Medicare's paying for? I want a cool white towel. Is it daytime? Nighttime? I'm burning up. My head is so ... Scooper? Are you still in the room? *(A pause.)*
SCOOPER.   I'm here.
HENNY.   I was going to tell you but I thought how can I tell him with so many worries so deep on his mind? Don't you think I know you're lonely? You got nobody in your life. Things aren't working out. I don't need optometrists to see all that. And now this. Nurses. Me coming home. Who's going to pay for it?
SCOOPER.   The Medicare takes it. Relax. When Jack died and you had that suicide —
HENNY.   It wasn't suicide. I reached for the wrong pills. I couldn't see. I thought they were breath fresheners. Life-Savers.

SCOOPER. Nobody takes eighty-six LifeSavers. Nobody's breath is that bad. Jack dying in one hospital. You suiciding in another. Me racing back and forth to see who'd die first. A five-day race. He went. You survived. When it was all over, the Medicare, for some reason I never followed up on, sent me a rebate of forty-four dollars. I made forty-four bucks off the two of you being in the hospital. Who knows what'll happen this time? Jackpot.
HENNY. How did I get in here so quickly? I thought hospitals had waiting lists. I thought you had to wait weeks to get appointments and beds. Three days ago you come see me and that very day I'm taken here and two days ago I'm operated on. How did we get in so quickly?
SCOOPER. It was an emergency.
HENNY. Pearl Harbor is an emergency. An old lady with female problems is no emergency. You didn't have to panic and carry me out.
SCOOPER. You were in pain. Why would you do that to yourself all these years? Put yourself in solitary confinement.
HENNY. Is there anyone else in the room?
SCOOPER. A lady over there. Asleep. Tubes coming out of her. Another lady was here. I guess being operated.
HENNY. Are they ack-blay?
SCOOPER. Both of them.
HENNY. Couldn't you get me a room with ite-whay people in it?
SCOOPER. You're lucky to have this room.
HENNY. Did you stick me on the charity ward?
SCOOPER. It's no charity ward.
HENNY. Let the nurses know I'm somebody. Tell them I am not run-of-the-mill. Tell them I used to be somebody.
SCOOPER. Who did you used to be?
HENNY. Make up somebody. You're the one who reads the books.
SCOOPER. Why don't you ever tell me the truth?
HENNY. Why don't you ever ask me the truth?
SCOOPER. Why did you try to kill yourself ten years ago?
HENNY. Why aren't you married?

SCOOPER. Why did you get married so late?
HENNY. Who is this Doctor James who got me in here?
SCOOPER. A doctor.
HENNY. What kind of a doctor?
SCOOPER. I don't know. He's — They have to be everything.
HENNY. Who does he look like?
SCOOPER. He looks like — believe it or not — he looks like Jack.
HENNY. My Jack? Your father?
SCOOPER. Same slicked-back hair.
HENNY. Your father. So embarrassed about his curls. I said Why God wasted curls on you. He said it was a present from heaven: beautiful brains. Doctor James looks like Jack? I can't wait for him to come in again.
SCOOPER. He won't. He's away.
HENNY. Jack could've had anybody. He had me. Biggest shock of my life when he said, Henny, give a guy a break. Marry me. He could've had any girl.
SCOOPER. What did Dad mean when he said "That's what I get for marrying a forty-two-year-old virgin." Why would you scream "I can't help it if I'm a good girl." Why would you scream over and over "I can't help it if I'm not a whore like your other women. I can't help it if I kept it for the man I married."
HENNY. I didn't realize I had given birth to a little cassette recorder.
SCOOPER. What kept you two together?
HENNY. I would've called you Xerox, bought stock in you and sold you.
SCOOPER. What was your life like before you married Jack? Before you had me? I'm almost the age you and Jack were when you met. What was your life like?
HENNY. Life like? Life like? Our life was lifelike. You like this Doctor James a lot. I can hear a blush in your voice.
SCOOPER. Did you ever have nightmares? You were thirty-eight, thirty-nine, forty. Alone. Unmarried.
HENNY. Your father and I went to dances.
SCOOPER. Why did two forty-year-old people get married for the first time?

HENNY. To hold up their pants? To get to the other side of the road? I'll bite. Why did two forty-year-old people get married for the first time? We had money to spend on ourselves. We were lonely. Is that a sin? To be lonely. My father had died. I was alone.
SCOOPER. How lonely were you?
HENNY. I met your father in a bar.
SCOOPER. Did it make you wake up in the middle of the night?
HENNY. We'd do this funny dance. I'd pull my bloomers down like a harem girl. We'd do this Egyptian dance.
SCOOPER. My father. Was he lonely?
HENNY. Why would he be lonely?
SCOOPER. You never asked him?
HENNY. I'm supposed to wake him up in the middle of the night and say to my husband I'm lucky to get "Are you lonely?" He'd thwack me on the head. A man is never lonely. A man on his deathbed can pick up the phone and get a date. A woman's different. I had buckteeth. They should've straightened my teeth while I was under the knife. They should've left my bosoms alone and broken my legs and reset them straight. I had gray hair when I was twenty-seven. Too honest to dye it. I made myself attractive telling jokes and acting the life of the party. Slaving in the kitchen. I was always afraid your father would leave. I was glad when he died. The worries were over. He couldn't leave me.
SCOOPER. Then why did you try to kill yourself?
HENNY. What are you? J. Edgar Hoover? Is this the Warren Commission?
SCOOPER. I'm trying to be honest.
HENNY. You just can't start being honest. You don't walk up to a fella and say Hey, today I'm honest.
SCOOPER. There must be something you want to know about me.
HENNY. I'm proud I never pried.
SCOOPER. You never knew how much money your own husband made.
HENNY. I waited for him to tell me.

SCOOPER. You didn't know how old he was.
HENNY. Not my business to ask.
SCOOPER. Your own husband?
HENNY. There was food on the table. You never went hungry.
SCOOPER. He didn't know how old you were.
HENNY. I was older. He would've left me.
SCOOPER. Two years older! Two years!
HENNY. Do they know here? How old I am?
SCOOPER. Your birthday's on your wrist in a little plastic tag.
HENNY. Take it off. Change the date!
SCOOPER. To what?
HENNY. Anything! Make it even older so they'll say I look swell for a ninety-five-year-old woman.
SCOOPER. You're going to die and I'm not going to know anything about you.
HENNY. You know enough about me
SCOOPER. How you felt?
HENNY. *(Angry.)* Felt? Felt? You make hats out of felt.
SCOOPER. I'm dying I'm so crazy. If I can straighten things out with you, maybe I can do it with all women —
HENNY. Don't you think I know you're unhappy? Don't you think I know that you know that I'm unhappy? You think I tried to kill myself for fun?
SCOOPER. That's the first time I ever heard you admit you tried to kill yourself. Did it hurt? There. That's a start. That's a start.
HENNY. I told the truth. Did the Red Sea part? I'm this old woman who does not want to live in the past and I have this son who is like living in a time capsule. They call it the past because it's over with, done, passed. Bury him with his copy of *Gone With the Wind*.
SCOOPER. You're going to be dead and I'm not going to know you.
HENNY. You put me in hospitals.
SCOOPER. Now? You blame me for this?
HENNY. You put me in hospitals before.
SCOOPER. You were crazy. You needed help.
HENNY. Causing blackouts all the electricity they put in me.

SCOOPER. You needed care.
HENNY. Whole coastlines blacked out because of me.
SCOOPER. No one could help you.
HENNY. Major cities. Industry crippled. Airlines. Television. Looting results because of the electricity they put in me to straighten out my head.
SCOOPER. You wouldn't trust anyone.
HENNY. Lot of good it did.
SCOOPER. You wouldn't listen to anyone. You wouldn't ask anyone anything.
HENNY. Okay. Who's this Doctor James that got me in here? I never heard you mention him before. I could hear the blush in your voice. As a kid you were a blusher. You're older. I bet your skin doesn't blush, but my ear is attuned to voices. I can hear the blush in your voice.
SCOOPER. Who do you think he is?
HENNY. What?
SCOOPER. I'm curious to know who you think he is.
HENNY. Twenty Questions? Don't you know? I think he's your —
SCOOPER. Speak up. Come on.
HENNY. I don't want the nurses to hear.
SCOOPER. To hear what?
HENNY. I think he's your boyfriend. Am I right?
SCOOPER. *(Laughing.)* Why do you think he's my boyfriend?
HENNY. My friend, Roberta Schildhauer, saw you at East Sixty-eighth Street where she was doing practical nursing across the street for a very wealthy lady and saw you going in and out of the building across the street. She asked the doorman who you went to visit.
SCOOPER. You don't need to see! You have a little blind person's Mafia.
HENNY. She told the doorman you were her daughter's ex-husband and owed alimony. The doorman said you went to see Doctor Virgil James. Roberta asked me who Doctor Virgil James was. I lied to her. I said Oh, an old college chum. They're scribbling away alumni notes.
SCOOPER. Doctor James is a psychiatrist.

HENNY. I know about these shrinkolas. They're all so cuckoo themselves I'm not surprised that's who you got mixed up with. Just don't let him give you drugs. There's nothing those mind shrinkers like better than getting you deep on the drugs. A man was on the Diane Sawyer show talking about how those mind shrinkers had screwed him up.
SCOOPER. He's my doctor.
HENNY. This man says in his book they're all junkies themselves.
SCOOPER. My doctor.
HENNY. Why don't you read nice books like that? Books I hear about on the radio that I could talk to you about. *You needing a psychiatrist?* You'd have to be an ingrate! Everything you got. A nice business.
SCOOPER. I'm selling the business. My share to Ted. All over. Finished. Can't work together anymore.
HENNY. Your best friends. Teddy and Valerie. They love you.
SCOOPER. Friends no more.
HENNY. They told me that. They called at Christmas. It's like a home for you.
SCOOPER. Like a home. I want my own home.
HENNY. Never be lonely with friends like that.
SCOOPER. I have been fucking Valerie for the past five years.
HENNY. They sent me flowers.
SCOOPER. She was going to leave Ted but at the last moment she developed this paralysis of the threshold. *(Pause.)*
HENNY. You and Valerie?
SCOOPER. That's carved on secret trees all over town.
HENNY. What about you and Doctor James?
SCOOPER. I'm his patient. *(She puts her hands over her face.)* You'd rather I were homosexual than had to go to a doctor?
HENNY. There's nothing sick in being homosexual.
SCOOPER. But going to a psychiatrist?
HENNY. That's sick. *(Scooper howls.)* I love to hear you laugh. When you laugh, the world's back in place. Laughter!! That's the best medicine! Laughter! Doctors know that'll put them out of business! Laugh, Scooper. *(Quiet.)* Scooper, are you here? *(A pause.)* Scooper?

SCOOPER. *(In agony.)* You've been in bughouses. I've had to put you there myself. I've seen you put in the back of trucks and taken away. You're up there in the Loony Hall of Fame. You have gold stars on your straitjackets. I've seen them.
HENNY. And a lot of good it did me. Psychiatrists. My son.
SCOOPER. Six years ago, your son found himself walking barefoot down Fifth Avenue in the dead of winter carrying a red plastic machine gun. Your son followed a young girl for five blocks because he knew she would be kidnapped and he had to protect her from the aliens who would kill her. Very Stephen King. Just in the nick of time, your son pulled this girl into a side street to let her know she was protected from those who would do harm to her hair and her skin and her fingernails. She screamed not knowing that your son was her savior. A passerby heard her scream and grabbed your son. Your son pulled the lit cigarette out of his lips and put it in the Good Samaritan's face. Your son ran down Fifth Avenue to the Gotham Book Mart that sells old books. Your son ran into the bookshop to find a different character for himself. Charles Dickens. Something with an eccentricity he could live with. The police got your son there. Took him to Bellevue. Thanks to Ted and Valerie, your son got transferred to the Psychiatric Institute here in this hospital. Your son's doctor was Doctor James, and he has been my doctor ever since.
HENNY. Did she press charges?
SCOOPER. No. But a few days later I got a book in the hospital. *The Letters of Mozart.* She had written inside "I am the girl you attacked. I want you to know I forgive you. Maybe a little contact with Mozart might heal you."
HENNY. I hope you sent her a thank you note.
SCOOPER. She didn't sign it. I had nowhere to send the letter. I loved those letters of Mozart.
HENNY. *(Groans.)* He loves the letters of Mozart.
SCOOPER. I said for years I look for the perfect girl. One day I snap. It all goes. I become a mugger. What do I do? I mug Miss Right. Nowhere to find her. I spent my time going after women to love them, to chase them, to hassle them, to talk to them, to touch them, to see them, to smell them, to feel them,

to wound them, to heal them, to taste them ...
HENNY.   Are you one of those transvestites?
SCOOPER.   No, Ma.
HENNY.   I hear about them on the radio. There's nothing wrong in being a transvestite.
SCOOPER.   I'm trying to clear my life out. I don't want to be crazy like you.
HENNY.   When you were eight years old, you put on my dress. And my makeup.
SCOOPER.   Maybe I was trying to find out who you were.
HENNY.   You could go on an afternoon talk show. Half man. Half woman. We made a joke. When you were being born we didn't know if we wanted a boy or a girl so we got a little bit of both.
SCOOPER.   I have this fantasy that one day you and I will have a scene that will clear everything out between us and I can lay you to rest while you're still alive.
HENNY.   Did you have one with your father?
SCOOPER.   Yes.
HENNY.   Oh no! You couldn't've. He was too busy fighting to share anything. Too busy ripping the tops off beer bottles. Bourbon bottles.
SCOOPER.   He had his stroke. I got a cab because that could come quicker than an ambulance.
HENNY.   I don't want to hear this.
SCOOPER.   He couldn't speak. Left leg couldn't move. Left arm. No voice. We drove up to this hospital. Over the Triborough Bridge. I held him in my arms. "All right, Jack," I said. "All right Dad. Everything is going to be great! Remember when I was a kid, Dad, and we'd ride over a bridge and you'd say 'You count all the boats on that side of the bridge, I count 'em on this side, whoever has the most is King for a Day!' Dad, I'll count boats for you. Six. Eight. Nine! You win! You're King for a Day! I love you, Dad." I told him that. I held him. I felt the right side of his body answer me.
HENNY.   Then I'll twitch and you can hold me and we'll call it quits.
SCOOPER.   Ma, feel these pajamas. Feel this robe. I'm not in

a seersucker suit. I'm a patient here. I got stabbed, Ma. In the spleen.
HENNY.   In the subway! I tell you to ride taxis! I tell you it's dangerous out there —
SCOOPER.   No muggers, Ma. I tried to hurt somebody again. The words all short-circuited. I didn't mean ... she didn't mean to.
HENNY.   Valerie? Ted stabbed you?
SCOOPER.   Deirdre.
HENNY.   Deirdre?
SCOOPER.   You don't know her.
HENNY.   That's what I tell Roberta Schildhauer. You got a million of them.
SCOOPER.   Why didn't you trust me? Why didn't you tell me? For two years why didn't you tell me you were standing in front of windows waving statues of impossible saints over you?
HENNY.   Where's the spleen?
SCOOPER.   I stay away from you because you are all chaos. Your body bursting open. I need my life structured, enclosed. I pick up a book. The page's rectangular shape, obvious but important, constant from book to book, dependable, the passion, wisdom, excitement captured in the center of the page tamed by the white margin. I lie on the rectangular couch of Doctor James and yes I become the words on the page. I can face my dreams.
HENNY.   Your father and I had that song we'd dance to. "I had a dream, dear, you had one too."
SCOOPER.   Ma, I have dreams that you picked me up and used me like a weapon against a strange man.
HENNY.   Where's the spleen?
SCOOPER.   I feel you holding my feet and my face so close to this strange man and my head is hitting his. My friendships with men are all fucked up. My friendships with women are all fucked up. The doctors say you can't live alone anymore.
HENNY.   Doctor James?
SCOOPER.   He's away. The surgeon said it.
HENNY.   No homes.
SCOOPER.   I can't take care of you.
HENNY.   Never asked you to.

SCOOPER. Why do you want to stay alive?
HENNY. Did I hear the question right? Why? Why!!!
SCOOPER. After devoting fifteen solid, very unsolid years to trying to bump yourself off —
HENNY. They were accidents! Household tragedies!
SCOOPER. Now when it's all over Why are you trying to hang on?
HENNY. It's not all over. You said they got it.
SCOOPER. They got it so it won't kill you immediately. They didn't go into the lymph glands. You couldn't have stood up to that. They got rid of the discomfort.
HENNY. How much ...
SCOOPER. What are you saying?
HENNY. Time.
SCOOPER. He said —
HENNY. Who said?
SCOOPER. The doctor said.
HENNY. I don't want any Doctor James said.
SCOOPER. The surgeon said.
HENNY. Get to it.
SCOOPER. In spite of everything, you were in remarkable health. He said the cancer —
HENNY. I hate that word.
SCOOPER. Could take ten years till it got you.
HENNY. Ten years?
SCOOPER. Ten years.
HENNY. Ten years! You gotta be joking: ten more years of this?
SCOOPER. Ten more years of this.
HENNY. I must be an awful burden to you.
SCOOPER. You're an awful burden to me.
HENNY. Ten years.
SCOOPER. *(Very quietly.)* Ma. In the drawer of the table to the right of your bed are your pills. Your sleeping pills. I put all your belongings into a plastic bag and put them in that drawer. Ma. You can't live in dignity. You have a chance right now to die in it.
HENNY. You want me to take the pills?

SCOOPER. I want you to take the pills.
HENNY. Are there enough?
SCOOPER. A lot.
HENNY. We'll do it?
SCOOPER. We'll do it.
HENNY. You won't feel badly?
SCOOPER. I won't feel badly.
HENNY. Give me the pills. *(Scooper looks around to make sure no one sees him take the pills out of her bedside table. He gives her the vial.)*
SCOOPER. Ma?
HENNY. Are these the pills?
SCOOPER. I loved you.
HENNY. Is this our scene?
SCOOPER. We'll give each other a hold.
HENNY. Don't do that. It hurts.
SCOOPER. Thank you.
HENNY. Thank you?
SCOOPER. For life. Caring for me.
HENNY. Oh, that.
SCOOPER. We'll forgive each other.
HENNY. You won't get into trouble over this?
SCOOPER. With your history?
HENNY. I don't want you getting into any trouble for this.
SCOOPER. Open your hands. *(He pours the pills in her palm.)*
HENNY. Give me water. *(He pours her water. She drinks.)* I'll need lots of water. It feels like a lot there. It's so exciting to drink water again. You're sure you won't get in trouble for this?
SCOOPER. I'll stay by your side. You'll fall asleep.
HENNY. To drink water and not have it burn.
SCOOPER. I'm by your side
HENNY. Water shouldn't burn.
SCOOPER. Still. Quiet.
HENNY. 350-2219. That's the butcher. He delivers. If you ever want anything delivered.
SCOOPER. 350-2219.
HENNY. I keep a hundred numbers right up here in my head.
SCOOPER. I loved you.

HENNY. I loved your father.
SCOOPER. Thank you. That's important to know.
HENNY. I love you.
SCOOPER. Good-bye.
HENNY. You sure you'll light a lot of candles for me?
SCOOPER. They'll see the glow in Helena, Montana.
HENNY. When I was a little girl, I dreamed of being a great actress and I would change my name to Helena Montana.
SCOOPER. Your own name is all right.
HENNY. Good-bye.
SCOOPER. Good-bye.
HENNY. *(Flings the pills across the room.)* You rotten little shit! Do you think they're going to let me bring killer pills in here? These are for my gas. You'd have done it? You'd have let me die?
SCOOPER. Take these pills! *(He picks them off the floor.)*
HENNY. Nurse! Nurse!
SCOOPER. Quiet. *(He turns to the door. He speaks to the nurse.)* She's all right. Was dreaming. *(He waits for the nurse to leave.)* I want you dead.
HENNY. God help me if I get gas in this hospital.
SCOOPER. What keeps you alive?
HENNY. You. I want to know what happens to you.
SCOOPER. *(Slumps to the floor.)* I want to kill you.
HENNY. That interests me.
SCOOPER. I want you to die.
HENNY. That, my God, amazes me.
SCOOPER. Nothing's working out for me.
HENNY. *(Thrilled.)* I know.
SCOOPER. *(Goes to his wheelchair.)* What am I going to do? I put all this time into Valerie.
HENNY. That's what I want to know about.
SCOOPER. What am I telling you? You can't help me.
HENNY. I'm not trying to.
SCOOPER. Ma, I'm not a book you sit there passively and keep turning the pages.
HENNY. Oh yes, you are. You're my book. The day the nurse put you in my arms, I looked down at you. This complete

stranger had come out of me. That I could produce this stranger. Would you take my breast? Would you drink? Would you live? Would you die? Would you be run over? Would you get polio or crib death or meningitis or be kidnapped? Would you learn? What would you look like? You've always come up trumps, Scooper. Just when I'm about to give up on you and I saw I knew what that boy is all about, out of the blue, I realize you're trying to kill me. That's so exciting. And to find out about you and Valerie! You could knock me over. Will she leave? Will she stay with Ted? How will Ted take it? Can you even keep Valerie? You want me to be open? Here I am. Open. But you're not ready to be. Poor Scooper.
SCOOPER. I'm not Scooper. My name is James.
HENNY. Now see that. I wondered how long you'd want to keep being called Scooper.
SCOOPER. You named me!
HENNY. I beg to differ. You were always scooping sand and putting it in your bucket. I said "You're like a little ostrich scooping sand for his head." You said "Scooper! Scooper!" You made us call you Scooper. If we wouldn't call you Scooper, you wouldn't come. It's awful having a kid with a silly name like Scooper. It could've been worse. You could've wanted to be called Ostrich. People would look at me as if actually calling another human being Scooper was my idea. Not my idea! His idea! Scooper. No wonder nobody can take you seriously. Or trust you. This is so interesting. I was wondering when you'd get around to changing your name back to what we named you. James! After my father. A wonderful man. James. The first. You're James the Second. *(Deirdre appears in the door. She has a robe over her hospital gown and hobbles in on crutches. Her foot is in a cast.)*
DEIRDRE. I called my father.
HENNY. Who's there?
DEIRDRE. I said a man tried to kill me.
HENNY. Who is that?
DEIRDRE. I said it fast so he wouldn't hang up on me. He didn't speak but he didn't hang up. I poured it all out. I told him I was in the hospital and I wouldn't be out to see him for

a few days and finally he spoke to me. He said "Give me his name. I will tell certain men to see him."
HENNY. Get out of my room. My son and I are —
DEIRDRE. "You don't touch a hair on the head of my Deirdre of the Sorrows." He said that.
HENNY. Is this for you, Scooper?
SCOOPER. Yes, Ma.
DEIRDRE. I said "Poppa, that's a play by John Millington Synge." He said "I named you after that play. Didn't I ever tell you?" He's going to kill you.
HENNY. Girl trouble?
SCOOPER. Yes, Ma.
HENNY. Scooper! *(She leans forward, concentrating intently.)*
DEIRDRE. He's going to send people out, find you and kill you for hurting the daughter of the professor. We talked! My father and I talked.
HENNY. Say something, Scooper!
SCOOPER. I think you're going to extremes. I'm very happy you and your father —
DEIRDRE. *(Hits the wheels of his chair with her crutches.)* Don't even mention him.
SCOOPER. You don't have to operate out of his code.
DEIRDRE. My father and I connected.
SCOOPER. You don't have to kill me to make up for all the years he didn't pay any attention to you.
DEIRDRE. I don't want his name in your mouth!
SCOOPER. You of all people should understand panic and losing control.
DEIRDRE. You did something worse. Worse than hitting me.
SCOOPER. You stabbed me.
HENNY. Stabbed! Scooper, this is wonderful!
DEIRDRE. Worse than making me stab you. Worse than screwing up Doctor James for me.
SCOOPER. In a way we had a wonderful afternoon. I had hoped we'd —
DEIRDRE. We'd what? You had your chance. You had me. You touched me. You dropped me.
SCOOPER. And you're going to have me killed?

DEIRDRE. You made me afraid. I want to find Doctor James. I want him to see you for what you are.
HENNY. Doctor James again! The Mystery Man!
SCOOPER. In a month you can tell him all.
DEIRDRE. Oh, I'll tell him all. He'll throw you out in the gutter if you ever show up there again.
SCOOPER. Tell him whatever you want. It's one way to finish with Doctor James.
DEIRDRE. *(Hits the wheels of his chair with her crutches.)* Don't you say one word against him.
SCOOPER. I don't know where he is.
DEIRDRE. How am I going to get through this goddamn month?
SCOOPER. I could put an emergency call into the AMA.
DEIRDRE. Who said April was the cruelest month?
SCOOPER. T. S. Eliot.
DEIRDRE. August. August. August.
HENNY. I know where he is. *(A pause.)*
DEIRDRE. Who is this woman?
HENNY. Hi! I'm him. But I don't want to butt in.
SCOOPER. What do you mean? You know where he is.
HENNY. When you went to check me in, we stood out on the sidewalk. Talk about heat. Sidewalks buckling beneath me. This strange hand holding on to me. I don't know where I am.
SCOOPER. What did he say?
HENNY. Don't get on the bed! You're worse than a cat! *(Scooper backs off.)* Is there such a place as Haiti?
DEIRDRE. Doctor James is in Haiti?
SCOOPER. Are you making this up?
HENNY. No! We were making conversation. I said New York's like a jungle. He said I'm going to the jungle. A big white hotel. Talk about creepy.
SCOOPER. Haiti! I could go there.
DEIRDRE. Haiti. I could go there.
SCOOPER. Talk to him.
DEIRDRE. Explain to him.
SCOOPER. He'd want to see me.
DEIRDRE. He'd weep to see me.

SCOOPER. I have the tickets.
DEIRDRE. I'll call my travel agent.
SCOOPER. I have the reservations at the same hotel. *(He takes his wallet out. He fishes out the airline tickets.)*
DEIRDRE. Fly down. See him. Fly right back. I could swing that.
SCOOPER. Take one ticket.
DEIRDRE. I don't want anything from you.
SCOOPER. Don't let it go to waste.
DEIRDRE. *(Takes the ticket.)* I'll pay you later.
SCOOPER. Fine.
DEIRDRE. I don't want any free rides.
SCOOPER. And none of us will ever get them.
DEIRDRE. He'll help us. He'll help you.
SCOOPER. He'll help you.
DEIRDRE. And I'm doomed to travel with you? It's like some plot.
SCOOPER. Shoes like a CIA agent. Not one crease in them. Silently sliding through our lives ... my God! You don't think —
DEIRDRE. It is a plot? You never mentioned to him you were going to Haiti?
SCOOPER. Haiti never came up.
DEIRDRE. And yet he knows. He's planned to drive us crazy all along. And bring us down there. He's arranged all this. Maybe he did it unconsciously. Even a shrink can have a subconscious. Doctor James is sitting under a palm tree. We're face to face. Finally. "So our little odyssey has brought us to the jungle ..."
SCOOPER. What is he trying to do to us?
DEIRDRE. That devil —
SCOOPER. That evil —
DEIRDRE. Diabolical.
SCOOPER. No. Good.
DEIRDRE. Wonderful.
SCOOPER. See him!
DEIRDRE. Face him! Knock on the door of his hotel room. She'll answer the door. "Oh, hello Mrs. James, may I see the doctor? It's Deirdre."

SCOOPER. "Hi Doctor. It's Scooper."
DEIRDRE. Scooper?
HENNY. Scooper. His name is Scooper. Not my idea.
DEIRDRE. I can't go into the jungle with anyone named Scooper.
HENNY. It's a nickname for James.
DEIRDRE. Your name is James? *(Pause.)*
SCOOPER. I never made the connection!!! Doctor James. Me James.
DEIRDRE. *(In awe.)* You've done it. You have devoured Dr. James. He is in you. The transference is complete. His wisdom has unlocked your wisdom. James. James!!! How lucky you are. *(She turns to go.)* Good-bye. *(Pause.)*
SCOOPER. Jane Bowles is neglected.
DEIRDRE. *(Stopping — but not turning.)* Carson McCullers.
SCOOPER. Joyce Carol Oates.
DEIRDRE. *(Turning.)* How can you say she's neglected? She writes a book a week.
SCOOPER. I never read them.
DEIRDRE. A neglected author is not one you choose to neglect. *(She turns to go.)*
SCOOPER. Joseph Conrad.
DEIRDRE. *Chance?*
SCOOPER. "Sacred call of life." Page 432.
DEIRDRE. Page 432. "The greatest sin to resist the embrace."
SCOOPER. Are we that couple?
DEIRDRE. I can't. I can't keep starting ...
SCOOPER. Your father — was he really in the Mafia?
DEIRDRE. He's a librarian.
SCOOPER. What's your truth?
DEIRDRE. Like everyone else's. Sordid, banal — of interest only to myself.
SCOOPER. Tell me one truth.
DEIRDRE. New York really is empty in August. *(Pause. Scooper stands. Deirdre motions him not to disturb Henny, who has fallen asleep. Scooper gestures to go outside. He pushes his wheelchair to the bed. Scooper and Deirdre go out. Henny wakes in the empty room.)*
HENNY. James? James? Is she gone? Take my hand, James?

(Pause.) OK. Play the Quiet Man. Hearing the name James over and over, I keep thinking of my father. He was a wonderful man. After he died, I was lost. His dying broke me in about a million pieces but after a while I pasted myself together into some kind of new teacup and toddled off to Boston for a new drink of water. I loved Boston. They laughed at my New York accent. It made me stand out. I met a man. Don Walker. He was Amish. I said "You must be nuts to love me." He said "No, because I have all my buttons." I said "Which makes you ex-Amish, seeing as how you are not allowed to have buttons." And he said "Well, you're no great shakes," and I said "Neither are you or you'd still be a Shaker." Believe me, it was funny at the time. We loved each other. I felt my father in heaven was paying attention to me and had sent Don to me as a heavenly present. But Don's Quaker mother who unfortunately was still on this earth would not have her precious ex-Amish son hitched up with a shanty Irish Catholic girl from Manhattan. Even though we were very lace curtain. Maybe rayon curtain. But not shanty. Not trash. But only a Quaker girl was good enough for her son. He buckled under. Stopped calling me. Neglected to keep dates. I got the message. I moved my broken teacup of a heart back to New York. Moved into 214 Riverside Drive. Met your father in the lobby. One disappointed person? Meet another disappointed person. Years went by. We got married. To show we could. We stayed together. We had you. And one day I dressed you up and got on the morning train to Boston. I waited outside my old office on Summer Street until Don Walker came out for lunch. I acted like I was just passing by. I wanted it to seem like I had just bumped into him, act casual, show him how great my life was, show off my beautiful child that was not his. And I saw him and I loved him so much. And after we said hellos and fancy meeting yous and acted surprised, I picked you up to show him what he missed and instead I hit him with you. Because he wasn't your father. Because he hadn't trusted me. Because I hadn't meant enough to him. I kept hitting him with you, pushing your face into his, till I realized your nose was bleeding. He was so shocked. I kept saying "You neglected me." I kept screaming like some shanty

Irish banshee: "I loved you." Finally he ran off. I wiped off your face. We got back on the next train to New York. Your father was home. He didn't ask why we were late, what we had done. He read his paper. Had his drinks. Slept. I put you to bed. I took off all my clothes and stood in front of the mirror. This body was not good enough. It couldn't get me what I wanted ... maybe if ... maybe ... I got dressed. Sat by your bed. Stared and stared at you. This was my prayer. A better life for you. You woke up. You looked at me. I want that for you. I want that for you ... James? *(She reaches out for her son.)*

CURTAIN

PROPERTY LIST

Empty mayonnaise jar (SCOOPER)
Juice jar (SCOOPER)
Box of Kotex (SCOOPER)
Wine and glasses (DEIRDRE)
Books and mailing box (DEIRDRE)
Books (SCOOPER)
Binoculars (DEIRDRE)
CD (DEIRDRE)
Picture in frame (DEIRDRE)
Wine bottle (DEIRDRE)
Book: Rilke's *Duino Elegies* (SCOOPER)
Book: Wodehouse's *Luck of the Bodkins* (SCOOPER)
Statue of Saint Jude (HENNY)
Cellular phone (SCOOPER)
Basin of water and bandages (DEIRDRE)
Cigarette (DEIRDRE)
Ashtray (DEIRDRE)
Suitcase (SCOOPER)
Rolodex (SCOOPER)
Paper knife (DEIRDRE)
Pitcher of water (SCOOPER)
Vial of pills (SCOOPER)
Glass (SCOOPER)

SOUND EFFECTS

Door chimes
Phone ringing

NEW PLAYS

- **SMASH by Jeffrey Hatcher.** Based on the novel, AN UNSOCIAL SOCIALIST by George Bernard Shaw, the story centers on a millionaire Socialist who leaves his bride on their wedding day because he fears his passion for her will get in the way of his plans to overthrow the British government. *"SMASH is witty, cunning, intelligent, and skillful."* –Seattle Weekly. *"SMASH is a wonderfully high-style British comedy of manners that evokes the world of Shaw's high-minded heroes and heroines, but shaped by a post modern sensibility."* –Seattle Herald. [5M, 5W] ISBN: 0-8222-1553-5

- **PRIVATE EYES by Steven Dietz.** A comedy of suspicion in which nothing is ever quite what it seems. *"Steven Dietz's ... Pirandellian smooch to the mercurial nature of theatrical illusion and romantic truth, Dietz's spiraling structure and breathless pacing provide enough of an oxygen rush to revive any moribund audience member ... Dietz's mastery of playmaking ... is cause for kudos."* –The Village Voice. *"The cleverest and most artful piece presented at the 21st annual [Humana] festival was PRIVATE EYES by writer-director Steven Dietz."* –The Chicago Tribune. [3M, 2W] ISBN: 0-8222-1619-1

- **DIMLY PERCEIVED THREATS TO THE SYSTEM by Jon Klein.** Reality and fantasy overlap with hilarious results as this unforgettable family attempts to survive the nineties. *"Here's a play whose point about fractured families goes to the heart, mind -- and ears."* –The Washington Post. *" ... an end-of-the millennium comedy about a family on the verge of a nervous breakdown ... Trenchant and hilarious ... "* –The Baltimore Sun. [2M, 4W] ISBN: 0-8222-1677-9

- **HONOUR by Joanna Murray-Smith.** In a series of intense confrontations, a wife, husband, lover and daughter negotiate the forces of passion, lust, history, responsibility and honour. *"Tight, crackling dialogue (usually played out in punchy verbal duels) captures characters unable to deal with emotions ... Murray-Smith effectively places her characters in situations that strip away pretense."* –Variety. *"HONOUR might just capture a few honors of its own."* –Time Out Magazine. [1M, 3W] ISBN: 0-8222-1683-3

- **NINE ARMENIANS by Leslie Ayvazian.** A revealing portrait of three generations of an Armenian-American family. *" ... Ayvazian's obvious personal exploration ... is evocative, and her picture of an American Life colored nostalgically by an increasingly alien ethnic tradition, is persuasively embedded into a script of a certain supple grace ... "* –The NY Post. *"... NINE ARMENIANS is a warm, likable work that benefits from ... Ayvazian's clear-headed insight into the dynamics of a close-knit family ... "* –Variety. [5M, 5W] ISBN: 0-8222-1602-7

- **PSYCHOPATHIA SEXUALIS by John Patrick Shanley.** Fetishes and psychiatry abound in this scathing comedy about a man and his father's argyle socks. *"John Patrick Shanley's new play, PSYCHOPATHIA SEXUALIS is ... perfectly poised between daffy comedy and believable human neurosis which Shanley combines so well ... "* –The LA Times. *"John Patrick Shanley's PSYCHOPATHIA SEXUALIS is a salty boulevard comedy with a bittersweet theme ... "* –New York Magazine. *"A tour de force of witty, barbed dialogue."* –Variety. [3M, 2W] ISBN: 0-8222-1615-9

DRAMATISTS PLAY SERVICE, INC.
440 Park Avenue South, New York, NY 10016 212-683-8960 Fax 212-213-1539
postmaster@dramatists.com www.dramatists.com

NEW PLAYS

• **A QUESTION OF MERCY** by David Rabe. The Obie Award-winning playwright probes the sensitive and controversial issue of doctor-assisted suicide in the age of AIDS in this poignant drama. *"There are many devastating ironies in Mr. Rabe's beautifully considered, piercingly clear-eyed work ..."* –The NY Times. *"With unsettling candor and disturbing insight, the play arouses pity and understanding of a troubling subject ... Rabe's provocative tale is an affirmation of dignity that rings clear and true."* –Variety. [6M, 1W] ISBN: 0-8222-1643-4

• **A DOLL'S HOUSE** by Henrik Ibsen, adapted by Frank McGuinness. Winner of the 1997 Tony Award for best revival. *"New, raw, gut-twisting and gripping. Easily the hottest drama this season."* –USA Today. *"Bold, brilliant and alive."* –The Wall Street Journal. *"A thunderclap of an evening that takes your breath away."* –Time. *"The stuff of Broadway legend."* –Associated Press. [4M, 4W, 2 boys] ISBN: 0-8222-1636-1

• **THE WAITING ROOM** by Lisa Loomer. Three women from different centuries meet in a doctor's waiting room in this dark comedy about the timeless quest for beauty -- and its cost. *"... THE WAITING ROOM ... is a bold, risky melange of conflicting elements that is ... terrifically moving ... There's no resisting the fierce emotional pull of the play."* –The NY Times. *"... one of the high points of this year's Off-Broadway season ... THE WAITING ROOM is well worth a visit."* –Back Stage. [7M, 4W, flexible casting] ISBN: 0-8222-1594-2

• **MR. PETERS' CONNECTIONS** by Arthur Miller. Mr. Miller describes the protagonist as existing in a dream-like state when the mind is "freed to roam from real memories to conjectures, from trivialities to tragic insights, from terror of death to glorying in one's being alive." With this memory play, the Tony Award and Pulitzer Prize-winner reaffirms his stature as the world's foremost dramatist. *"... a cross between Joycean stream-of-consciousness and Strindberg's dream plays, sweetened with a dose of William Saroyan's philosophical whimsy ... CONNECTIONS is most intriguing ... Miller scholars will surely find many connections of their own to make between this work and the author's earlier plays."* –The NY Times. [5M, 3W] ISBN: 0-8222-1687-6

• **THE STEWARD OF CHRISTENDOM** by Sebastian Barry. A freely imagined portrait of the author's great-grandfather, the last Chief Superintendent of the Dublin Metropolitan Police. *"MAGNIFICENT ... the cool, elegiac eye of James Joyce's THE DEAD; the bleak absurdity of Samuel Beckett's lost, primal characters; the cosmic anger of KING LEAR ..."* –The NY Times. *"Sebastian Barry's compassionate imaging of an ancestor he never knew is among the most poignant onstage displays of humanity in recent memory."* –Variety. [5M, 4W] ISBN: 0-8222-1609-4

• **SYMPATHETIC MAGIC** by Lanford Wilson. Winner of the 1997 Obie for best play. The mysteries of the universe, and of human and artistic creation, are explored in this award-winning play. *"Lanford Wilson's idiosyncratic SYMPATHETIC MAGIC is his BEST PLAY YET ... the rare play you WANT ... chock-full of ideas, incidents, witty or poetic lines, scientific and philosophical argument ... you'll find your intellectual faculties racing."* –New York Magazine. *"The script is like a fully notated score, next to which most new plays are cursory lead sheets."* –The Village Voice. [5M, 3W] ISBN: 0-8222-1630-2

DRAMATISTS PLAY SERVICE, INC.
440 Park Avenue South, New York, NY 10016 212-683-8960 Fax 212-213-1539
postmaster@dramatists.com www.dramatists.com